ULTIMATE
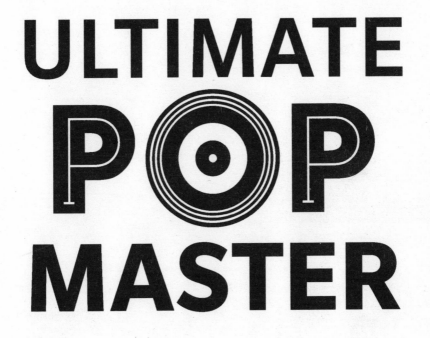
MASTER

ULTIMATE

POP
MASTER

**Phil Swern and
Neil Myners**

Foreword by
Ken Bruce

BOOKS

1

BBC Books, an imprint of Ebury Publishing, 20 Vauxhall Bridge Road, London SW1V 2SA

BBC Books is part of the Penguin Random House group of companies whose addresses can be found at global.penguinrandomhouse.com

Penguin
Random House
UK

This book is published to accompany the BBC Radio Two quiz show *PopMaster*, broadcast on *The Ken Bruce Show*

First published by BBC Books in 2020

www.penguin.co.uk

A CIP catalogue record for this book is available from the British Library

ISBN 9781785944987

Printed and bound in Great Britain by Clays Ltd, Elcograf S.p.A.

Penguin Random House is committed to a sustainable future for our business, our readers and our planet. This book is made from Forest Stewardship Council® certified paper.

MIX
Paper from
responsible sources
FSC® C018179

C◉NTENTS

F◉REWORD

'PopMaster' began on my daily show on Radio 2 back in 1996 when I was looking for a couple of new features to include in order to freshen up the morning programme. Along with my producer at the time, Colin Martin, and question setter Phil Swern, we went out for a mighty fine lunch and, after several hours, came up with the idea of 'PopMaster'.

Once it was launched, we thought it would probably run for 13 weeks or so but, to everyone's amazement, it gradually became one of the high spots of the show. Over the years the audience has grown and grown, culminating into what has now become the most listened to half hour every weekday morning on the entire Radio 2 network.

The quiz took to the road for the first time in 2013, raising money for *BBC Children in Need*, for which we have done subsequent events. We followed that up with other live and corporate events and hopefully we'll run many more in the future; we're also planning a nationwide quiz in selected pubs around the country, so keep an eye out for one near you.

In 2014, the first *PopMaster* book was published, which managed to find its way into the bestsellers so another was commissioned for the following year, and I'm pleased to note that also found similar success. However, there hasn't been a new book since then so I was delighted when we were able to approach Penguin Random House with a view to bringing out a brand spanking new edition with a completely fresh look and a more user-friendly layout.

I really hope you enjoy playing along with the questions set here by our regular question setters, Neil Myners and Phil (The Collector) Swern and hope you score well as you turn the pages of this very fine new-look *PopMaster* book. If you haven't already, please join me every weekday morning at 10.30 on Radio 2 and, who knows, maybe you'll be one of our lucky contestants!

Ken Bruce, BBC Radio 2

HOW IT WORKS

The following pages may very well test your pop brain to its limit. How strong is your musical mental pain threshold? At what point will you crack?

Fear not, we're here to make this a pleasant rather than a tortuous experience. We've devised what will hopefully be an enjoyable romp through chart knowledge and trivia.

We've divided this book into five sections – Top 50, Top 40, Top 30, Top 20 and Top 10. As you work your way through, you'll find that some questions need a little more thought. Answers can be found overpage – for example, if you're looking for the answers to Quiz 1, they will be underneath Quiz 2, and so on.

Think of the Top 50 as a musical equivalent to your standard gym warm-up (if that is your thing!). After this, we'll explain the contents of each section as you come to it. But it ends with sets of questions familiar to regular listeners of Ken Bruce's show – a Top 10 section of questions similar to those faced by Ken's 'Champion of Champions' contestants.

We really hope you enjoy this book and that along the way you pick up some interesting nuggets of trivia you might not have read or heard about before.

And if any of the quizzes keep you awake at night searching for the answer? Well, don't shoot us, we're only the question writers!

Phil Swern & Neil Myners

OK! We're Off!

Here's your warm-up section to get you in the mood for some more challenging rounds later in the book. The questions in this section are just like the ones Ken would ask on air, but there are a few tricky ones thrown in for good measure along the way. It would be a bit dull to score maximum points all the way through, wouldn't it?

TOP
50

QUIZ **1**

Which multi-platinum selling artist topped the singles chart in 2011 with her song 'Someone Like You'?

Madness achieved two Top 10 hits with the word 'House' in the title, one was 'Our House', what was the other?

Which group reached number one in 1976 with the song 'December, 1963 (Oh, What A Night)'?

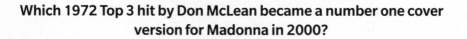

Which 1972 Top 3 hit by Don McLean became a number one cover version for Madonna in 2000?

The English producer who made the Top 10 in 1999 with his arrangement of 'Barber's Adagio For Strings' is called William... who?

What do the letters P and J stand for in singer PJ Harvey's name?

Avril Lavigne scored her first hit in 2002, what was the title?

Who duetted with Celine Dion on the 1992 hit movie theme from *Beauty and the Beast*?

Released in 1964, The Moody Blues had their only number one single early in 1965 with which song?

In 1988, the song 'Tell It To My Heart' was the first and biggest UK hit for which American female singer?

QUIZ **2**

1

What are the names of both of the members of Pet Shop Boys?

2

The trio Peter, Paul and Mary achieved their only UK Top 10 hit in 1970 – what was the title?

3

Who reached No. 1 in 1992 with 'Sleeping Satellite'?

4

Complete the title of this 1994 Top 10 hit by Morrissey: 'The More You Ignore Me, …' what?

5

Which group of comedians had a Top 20 hit in 1975 with 'Black Pudding Bertha (The Queen of Northern Soul)'?

6

Which legendary soul singer is the subject of a 2015 No. 1 hit by Charlie Puth featuring Meghan Trainor?

7

Who's '(Re-version)' of the 'James Bond Theme' was a Top 10 hit in 1997 and featured on the soundtrack to *Tomorrow Never Dies*?

8

The voice of which former Radio 1 DJ can be heard on the 1991 single 'Radio Wall of Sound' – the final original Top 40 hit single for Slade?

9

During the 1990s, the group Hanson had three Top 10 singles but only one topped the charts. What was the title?

10

What was the title of the 1984 debut Top 10 hit by Julian Lennon?

TOP **50**

ANSWERS QUIZ **1**

1. Adele 2. 'House of Fun' 3. Four Seasons 4. 'American Pie' 5. Orbit 6. Polly Jean 7. 'Complicated' 8. Peabo Bryson 9. 'Go Now!' 0. Taylor Dayne

QUIZ **3**

What is the title of Bruce Springsteen's Top 10 seasonal song from 1985?

Which TV presenters made the Top 3 in 2002 with 'We're on the Ball', the official song of the England football team?

What shared song title provided different Top 10 singles for Clodagh Rodgers in 1971 and the Moments in 1977?

'Another Way to Die' sung by Jack White and Alicia Keys is the title song to which James Bond movie?

Which other American rapper was featured on Warren G's 1994 Top 5 hit 'Regulate'?

6

Released in 1989, 'The Magic Number' and 'Buddy' was a Top 10 double 'A' sided hit at the start of 1990 for which rap trio?

7

Who had a No. 1 song for nine weeks in 2018 called 'God's Plan'?

8

In the 1980s, the song 'Saturday Love' was a Top 10 duet for Cherrelle with Alexander O'Neal, but they had a second hit duet that decade billed as Alexander O'Neal featuring Cherrelle – what was that second hit called?

9

Which group had Top 20 hits in the mid-1960s with the songs 'What Have They Done to the Rain' and 'Take Me for What I'm Worth'?

10

Which *X Factor* winner reached No. 1 in 2010 with the song 'When We Collide'?

QUIZ 4

(((1)))

The 1999 Top 3 hit 'What I Am' by Tin Tin Out featured which female vocalist?

(((2)))

What was the name of the record label formed by Elton John during the 1970s?

(((3)))

Which rapper was featured on Katy Perry's 2010 No. 1 hit, 'California Gurls'?

(((4)))

Dion had a Top 20 hit with 'Runaround Sue' in 1961 but what was the title of the even more successful follow up from the following year?

(((5)))

Genesis made the Top 10 in 1982 with their '3X3' EP – can you name any one of the three songs included on the record?

(((6)))

Featuring Puff Daddy and Ma$e, which American rapper achieved a Top 10 hit in 1997 with 'Mo Money Mo Problems'?

(((7)))

Including Dave Edmunds in their line-up, which band's only hit was a 1968 rock version of Khachaturian's 'Sabre Dance'?

(((8)))

Which *Britain's Got Talent* runner-up made her solo chart debut with the Top 10 hit, 'Wild Horses'?

(((9)))

What was the title of the only No. 1 hit single achieved by the Bachelors?

(((10)))

What is the title of the Ed Sheeran album that contains the No. 1s 'Thinking Out Loud' and 'Sing' as well as the Top 3 hit 'Bloodstream'?

QUIZ **5**

What was the title of the first single by Oasis to make the Top 10?

Released in 1974, which brother and sister act had a Top 5 single early in 1975 with 'Morning Side of the Mountain'?

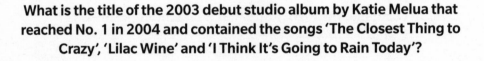

What is the title of the 2003 debut studio album by Katie Melua that reached No. 1 in 2004 and contained the songs 'The Closest Thing to Crazy', 'Lilac Wine' and 'I Think It's Going to Rain Today'?

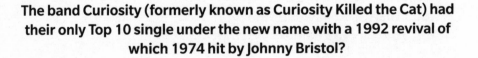

The band Curiosity (formerly known as Curiosity Killed the Cat) had their only Top 10 single under the new name with a 1992 revival of which 1974 hit by Johnny Bristol?

Who had a No. 1 in 2009 with 'My Life Would Suck Without You'?

According to his 2010 Top 10 hit, who claimed 'She's Always a Woman' on his cover version of the Billy Joel song?

Name the Scottish rock band that successfully revived Cameo's 1986 single 'Word Up' for a Top 10 hit in 1994.

Topol's 1967 Top 10 song 'If I Were a Rich Man' came from which successful musical?

Can you name the R&B group that made the Top 5 in 2001 with their hits 'All I Want' and 'One Night Stand'?

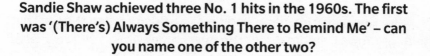

Sandie Shaw achieved three No. 1 hits in the 1960s. The first was '(There's) Always Something There to Remind Me' – can you name one of the other two?

ANSWERS QUIZ **4**

1. Emma Bunton 2. Rocket 3. Snoop Dogg 4. 'The Wanderer' (Top 10 in 1962 and Top 20 when re-released in 1976) 5. 'Paperlate' (lead track and airplay hit), 'You Might Recall', 'Me and Virgil' 6. The Notorious B.I.G. 7. Love Sculpture 8. Susan Boyle 9. 'Diane' 10. × ('Multiply')

QUIZ **6**

What was the title of the Spice Girls' debut No. 1 hit?

What was the title of the only Top 10 hit achieved by husband and wife duo Womack and Womack?

What is the name of the singer who suggested we 'Kiss the Rain' according to the title of her 1988 Top 5 single?

Procol Harum were partly formed by members of which 1960s group that achieved one Top 40 hit in 1964 with 'Poison Ivy'?

Name the short-lived Irish boyband of the late 1990s that had Top 20 singles with their versions of the Osmonds 'Let Me In' and Air Supply's 'All Out of Love'.

In 1978, Heatwave made the Top 10 with their double 'A' sided hit 'Always and Forever' and which other song?

What was the title of the only UK No. 1 single by the Supremes?

8

Name the dance act that topped the charts in 1995 with their hits 'Don't Stop (Wiggle Wiggle)' and 'Boom Boom Boom'.

9

What is the title of the album by Little Mix that contains the tracks 'Shout Out to My Ex,' 'Nobody Like You' and 'No More Sad Songs'?

10

Name the group whose hits in the late 1960s included 'Helule Helule', 'My Little Lady' and 'Hello World'.

TOP **50**

ANSWERS QUIZ 5

1. 'Live Forever' (No. 10 in 1994) 2. Donny and Marie Osmond 3. Call Off the Search 4. 'Hang on in There Baby' (both versions peaked at No. 3) 5. Kelly Clarkson 6. Fyfe Dangerfield 7. Gun 8. *Fiddler on the Roof* 9. Mis-Teeq 10. 'Long Live Love'; 'Puppet on a String' (all three songs spent three weeks at No. 1)

QUIZ **7**

What was the title of the Top 10 debut chart appearance by Glen Campbell in the UK?

What is the title of the album by Queen that includes the tracks 'The Invisible Man', 'Rain Must Fall' and 'Scandal'?

Which superstar set up the Paisley Park record label in the 1980s?

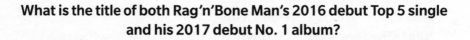

What is the title of both Rag'n'Bone Man's 2016 debut Top 5 single and his 2017 debut No. 1 album?

Can you name the singer who made the Top 10 in 1998 with 'Searchin' My Soul', the title song to the TV series *Ally McBeal*?

Name the act that reached No. 1 in 1989 with 'Swing the Mood'.

What was the name of the successful band formed in 1966 by Jack Bruce, Eric Clapton and Ginger Baker?

Which group's Top 10 hits included 'Common People', 'Something Changed' and 'Disco 2000'?

Which American singer's 1999 Top 10 hit 'I Try' went on to be a hit in the US the following year, and won her a Grammy for 'Best Female Pop Vocal Performance'?

Name the rock band that made the Top 20 in 1970 with their only Top 40 single 'Who Do You Love'.

ANSWERS QUIZ **6**

1. 'Wannabe' 2. 'Teardrops' (No. 3 in 1988) 3. Billie Myers 4. The Paramounts 5. OTT 6. 'Mind Blowing Decisions' 7. 'Baby Love' 8. The Outhere Brothers 9. *Glory Days* 10. The Tremeloes

QUIZ **8**

1

Released in 1979, who duetted with Syreeta on 'With You I'm Born Again', a Top 5 hit in early 1980?

2

What does the MFSB stand for in the name of the act that made the Top 40 in 1974 with 'TSOP (The Sound of Philadelphia)'?

3

Which of these hit singles by the vocal group Honeyz was both their 1998 chart debut and also their highest charting single – 'Love of a Lifetime', 'Finally Found' or 'I Don't Know'?

4

What was the name of the act that made the UK Top 10 in 1967 with 'Snoopy vs The Red Baron'?

5

Which singer was joined by the Kumars on the 2003 No. 1, 'Spirit in the Sky'?

6

The Nashville Teens achieved two Top 10 hits in the 1960s, the first being 'Tobacco Road', but what was the second?

7

Busta Rhymes made his Top 10 debut in 1996 with which single?

8

From 1985, what was the name of the artist whose only hit single was 'Tarzan Boy'?

9

Who is the female vocalist featured on the Communards' 1986 No. 1 hit 'Don't Leave Me This Way'?

10

Which group's last Top 10 hit in the 1970s was the 1973 Top 3 song 'Alright, Alright, Alright'?

TOP **50**

ANSWERS QUIZ **7**

1. 'Wichita Lineman' 2. *The Miracle* 3. Prince 4. 'Human' 5. Vonda Shepard 6. Jive Bunny and the Mastermixers 7. Cream 8. Pulp 9. Macy Gray 10. Juicy Lucy

QUIZ **9**

Who had Top 40 hits in the 1970s with 'Can't Keep It In', 'Moon Shadow' and 'Another Saturday Night'?

Released in 1991 and featuring guest vocals by Kate Pierson of the B-52s, what is the title of the first Top 10 single achieved by R.E.M.?

Who had a Top 10 hit in 1976 with the movie version of 'Pinball Wizard' from the musical *Tommy*?

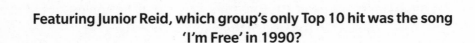

Featuring Junior Reid, which group's only Top 10 hit was the song 'I'm Free' in 1990?

In December 2002, S Club Juniors made the Top 10 with a double 'A' sided hit – one side was 'Puppy Love' but what was the title of the other?

In which successful group was Ray Parker Jr a member prior to his solo hits?

(MC Sar &) Real McCoy had two Top 10 hits in the 1990s – the first was 'Another Night' but what was the title of the other?

(((8)))

'Maneater' was a Top 10 single for Daryl Hall & John Oates in 1982, but which singer reached No. 1 with a song that shares that same title in 2006?

(((9)))

According to their 1970 hit, T.Rex wanted to 'Ride ...' what?

(((10)))

Which Dutch group in 1998 suggested we had 'Sex on the Beach' in the title of their Top 3 single?

QUIZ **10**

1

Otis Redding achieved just one Top 10 hit during the 1960s – what was the title?

2

Which actress duetted with Robbie Williams on the 2001 version of 'Somethin' Stupid'?

3

Originally featured on their 1968 album *Beggars Banquet*, what type of '… Man' did the Rolling Stones sing about on the group's 1971 single?

4

Can you name Billy Joel's former wife who was featured in the video of his No. 1 single 'Uptown Girl'?

5

In 2018, which American band reached the Top 3 with the song 'Feel It Still'?

6

Led by songwriter Paddy McAloon, which group had hits in the 1990s with the songs 'A Prisoner of the Past', 'The Sound of Crying' and 'Jordan: The EP'?

7

Which 1973 Top 10 single by George Harrison has the subtitle '(Give Me Peace on Earth)'?

8

What was the title of the first Top 10 hit achieved by Eurythmics?

((9))

Which one of these hit singles by Roy Orbison reached No. 1 – 'Running Scared,' 'It's Over' or 'In Dreams'?

((10))

The Top 10 song 'I Love My Radio (My Dee Jay's Radio)' was the only Top 40 hit for which UK female singer in the 1980s?

ANSWERS QUIZ **9**

1. Cat Stevens 2. 'Shiny Happy People' 3. Elton John 4. The Soup Dragons 5. 'Sleigh Ride' 6. Raydio 7. 'Run Away' 8. Nelly Furtado 9. 'A White Swan' 10. T-Spoon

QUIZ **11**

1

Name the band who made the Top 10 in 1997 with a cover of the Ohio Players' 1975 American No. 1 'Love Rollercoaster'.

2

Which of these No. 1s by S Club 7 was the first to make the charts: 'Don't Stop Movin'', 'Bring It All Back' or 'Never Had a Dream Come True'?

3

Can you name the group that made the Top 20 in 1970 with 'Gasoline Alley Bred'?

4

Which shared title has provided both the band Cast with a Top 10 song in 1996 and the Finnish DJ & producer Darude with a Top 3 trance instrumental in 2000?

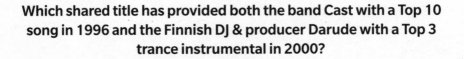

5

Who was credited with playing trumpet on Modern Romance's 1982 Top 20 hit 'Cherry Pink and Apple Blossom White'?

What type of '... Man' did the Smiths sing about on the group's 1983 debut hit?

With whom did Glen Campbell duet on a 1969 version of the Everly Brothers' hit 'All I Have to Do Is Dream'?

To which actor did Madness pay tribute on one of their 1984 Top 20 hits?

Having already had seven Top 40 hits, which band first reached the Top 10 in 1999 with the song 'Why Does It Always Rain On Me?'?

In 1985, the Commodores had their only UK Top 10 single since the departure of Lionel Richie from the group – what is it called?

QUIZ **12**

1

The 1971 Top 3 song 'Co-Co' was the first of ten Top 10 singles for which glam-rock group?

2

From 1993, what was the title of the only Top 10 single for the Beloved?

3

Featured in the 1937 film *Way Out West*, which duo made the Top 3 in 1975 with 'The Trail of the Lonesome Pine'?

4

Which singer-songwriter was in the Top 10 in January 2017 with 'September Song'?

5

Which song has been both a Top 10 hit for Cyndi Lauper in 1989 and a posthumous Top 10 hit for Roy Orbison in 1992?

6

Now You See Me ... Now You Don't, *Always Guaranteed* and *Stronger* were all Top 10 albums in the 1980s for which legendary singer?

7

What was the name of the record label launched by Led Zeppelin in 1974 to release their own material?

Name the group that had No. 1s in 1999 with 'Boom, Boom, Boom, Boom!!' and 'We're Going to Ibiza!'.

What was the title of the 1988 Top 20 hit by Patrick Swayze featuring Wendy Fraser that was included in the movie *Dirty Dancing*?

Which soulful British boyband had a Top 10 single in 1999 with 'From the Heart', which featured on the soundtrack to the film *Notting Hill*?

ANSWERS QUIZ **11**

1. The Red Hot Chili Peppers 2. 'Bring It All Back' (1999 debut hit; Never Had a Dream Come True', 2000; 'Don't Stop Movin'', 2001) 3. The Hollies 4. 'Sandstorm' 5. John Du Prez 6. 'This Charming Man' 7. Bobbie Gentry 8. Michael Caine 9. Travis 10. 'Nightshift'

QUIZ **13**

Having already had eight Top 40 singles, 'The Eton Rifles' was the first Top 10 hit for which successful band?

What is the name of the singer who duetted with Paul Young on the 1991 Top 5 hit 'Senza Una Donna (Without a Woman)'?

What was the title of the only Top 10 song of the 1960s by the Beatles not to have been written by John Lennon and Paul McCartney?

Who had a Top 10 hit in 1994 with the title song to his TV drama series *Crocodile Shoes*?

Name the German act that took a techno version Supertramp's 'The Logical Song' into the charts in 2002.

From 1999, what is the title of the chart debut and first Top 10 hit for Eminem?

In 2012, who suggested we 'Turn Up the Music' on his No. 1 song?

Which 1964 Top 20 hit by Elvis Presley was a Top 10 cover for ZZ Top in 1992?

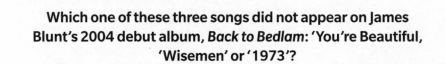

Which one of these three songs did not appear on James Blunt's 2004 debut album, *Back to Bedlam*: 'You're Beautiful, 'Wisemen' or '1973'?

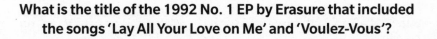

What is the title of the 1992 No. 1 EP by Erasure that included the songs 'Lay All Your Love on Me' and 'Voulez-Vous'?

QUIZ 14

1 Which group had No. 1s in the 1970s called 'Tiger Feet', 'Lonely This Christmas' and 'Oh Boy'?

2 With which group have Jet Harris, Bruce Welch and Tony Meehan all been members?

3 Which female singer with hits in the 1960s featured on the Audio Bullys' 2005 Top 3 single 'Shot You Down'?

4 What was the title of the 1972 debut hit for Roxy Music?

5 Who wrote and recorded the 1987 Top 5 single '(Something Inside) So Strong'?

6 In December 1995, Mike Flowers Pops reached No. 2 with a song that had originally been No. 2 for Oasis the previous month – what is the song?

7 ... and which American artist took his version of the answer to the previous question into the Top 40 in 2004?

8 With which successful chart act do you most associate singer Gwen Dickey?

In 1999, Westlife had the Christmas No. 1 with a double 'A' sided single that featured cover versions of the 1974 No. 1 'Seasons in the Sun' and which 1979 song by Abba?

10

Which American singer had a Top 3 hit in 1961 with the double 'A' sided single 'Hello Mary Lou' and 'Travelin' Man'?

TOP **50**

QUIZ **15**

Which boyband topped the charts in 2003 with their singles 'You Said No' and 'Crashed the Wedding'?

Who wrote and produced Mott the Hoople's first hit, 'All The Young Dudes'?

What was the title of the Hollies' only No. 1 hit single of the 1960s?

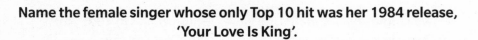

Name the female singer whose only Top 10 hit was her 1984 release, 'Your Love Is King'.

Which member of Sugababes duetted with George Michael on his 2006 Top 20 song 'This Is Not Real Love'?

What was the title of the 1987 Top 3 song by Tom Jones that was featured in the musical *Matador*?

Who first reached No. 1 in the spring of 2000 with his single 'Fill Me In'?

What was the title of the only single by Johnny Mathis to make the Top 10 during the 1960s?

Name the act that in 1996 entered the charts at No. 1 with a cover of the Bee Gees' song 'How Deep Is Your Love'.

Two singles by Sister Sledge were originally hits in 1979, then both in the charts again as remixes in 1984, and then once again as second remixes in 1993. 'We Are Family' is one of these two songs – what is the other?

QUIZ **16**

1

Who sang about 'Supermarket Flowers' on his 2017 hit?

2

What were 'Ever Changing' according to the title of the Style Council's 1984 Top 5 song ?

3

In what movie was Maria McKee's 1990 No. 1 hit 'Show Me Heaven' featured?

4

Which of these three Guns N' Roses hits achieved the highest chart placing: 'Nightrain', 'Welcome to the Jungle' or 'November Rain'?

5

Which group's only Top 10 hit was their 1991 Top 3 song 'More Than Words'?

6

What is the name of singer Eydie Gormé's husband who duetted with her on the 1963 Top 3 hit 'I Want to Stay Here'?

7

From 1978, what was the title of the only Top 10 hit achieved by Frankie Miller?

8

Which one of these three songs did not appear on Dire Straits' album *Brothers in Arms*: 'So Far Away', 'Romeo & Juliet', 'Your Latest Trick'?

9

According to his 2016 No. 2 hit, who was 'Dancing on My Own'?

10

What was the title of the only No. 1 hit single for B. Bumble and the Stingers in 1962?

ANSWERS QUIZ **15**

1. Busted 2. David Bowie 3. 'I'm Alive' 4. Sade 5. Mutya Buena (billed as George Michael and Mutya) 6. 'A Boy from Nowhere' 7. Craig David 8. 'My Love for You' 9. Take That 10. 'Lost in Music' (a third single, 'Thinking of You', was a hit in 1984 and 1993, but not in 1979)

QUIZ **17**

What were Bon Jovi 'Livin' on ...' according to their only single in the 1980s to reach the Top 10?

Which group made their chart debut in 1967 with the Top 3 song 'Night of Fear' and followed this with a Top 5 hit the same year called 'I Can Hear the Grass Grow'?

According to their 1979 Top 3 hit, which group found themselves 'Up the Junction'?

Van Halen in the 1980s, Kriss Kross in the 1990s and Madonna in the 2000s have all had Top 10 hits with different songs that share the same title – what is that title?

Which American singer and actor had hits in the second half of the 1970s with 'Let's Have a Quiet Night in' and 'It Sure Brings Out the Love in Your Eyes'?

From 1983, what was the title of the only No. 1 hit for KC and the Sunshine Band?

Which female singer had a Top 20 hit in 1992 with 'The World Is Stone', as featured in the movie *Tycoon*?

Which dance act made the Top 10 in the 1980s with 'Superfly Guy' and 'Hey Music Lover'?

Carole King composed which 1971 Top 5 hit recorded by James Taylor?

According to their 1999 No. 1 hit, which duo were 'Sweet Like Chocolate'?

QUIZ 18

1

Michael Ball and Climie Fisher had different Top 3 hits in the late 1980s with similarly titled songs – what are they both called?

2

In 1978, the American band Exile had its only Top 40 hit with which Top 10 song?

3

Which female singer achieved Top 10 hits in the early 1960s with the singles 'Little Miss Lonely' and 'Tell Me What He Said'?

4

Who sang about an 'Air Balloon' on her Top 10 song in 2014?

5

In 2000, the Spice Girls topped the charts for the ninth time with a double 'A' sided hit; one song was 'Holler', but what was the other?

6

The 1974 hit 'Long Legged Woman Dressed in Black' was the title of the eighth and final Top 40 single by which group?

7

Which of these three Top 10 hits by Ronan Keating was the only one to reach No. 1: 'Life Is a Rollercoaster,' 'The Way You Make Me Feel' or 'Lost for Words'?

8

The songs 'Swear It Again' in 1999 and 'The Rose' in 2006 are the titles of the first and last of 14 No. 1s for which group?

9

What was the title of the only 1970s solo Top 10 hit achieved by Roger Daltrey?

10

Who had hits in the 1980s with the songs 'Wouldn't It Be Good' and 'Wide Boy'?

TOP **50**

QUIZ **19**

Diana Ross recorded the 1974 hit duets 'You Are Everything' and 'Stop Look Listen (to Your Heart)' with which legendary soul singer?

Which American outlaw featured in the title of a 1990 hit single by Cher?

According to their 2003 Top 20 hit, which band's maths worked out that '2 +2 = 5'?

Which one of these three Gary Numan hits gained the highest chart position: 'Complex', 'This Wreckage' or 'Music for Chameleons'?

With which group of the 1990s and early 2000s do you most associate Jarvis Cocker?

Wizzard achieved two No. 1 hits during the 1970s – the first was 'See My Baby Jive', but what was the title of the other?

Which major Petula Clark hit was composed by Charlie Chaplin?

Name the duo that reached No. 1 in 1992 with 'Would I Lie to You'.

What was the title of the debut hit and only No. 1 for Emile Ford & the Checkmates?

Who was featured on will.i.am's 2014 No. 1 hit 'It's My Birthday'?

QUIZ **20**

1

What was the title of the only single by INXS to make the Top 10 during the 1980s?

2

Which singer had Top 10 hits in the 1960s with 'Chain Gang', 'Twistin' the Night Away' and 'Cupid'?

3

Which song has been a Top 20 hit in 1982 for Robert Palmer, for Rod Stewart in 1984 and for Maxi Priest in 1987?

4

Which female singer featured on East 17's 1996 Top 3 hit 'If You Ever'?

5

Name the singer who entered the charts at No. 1 in 2013 with her hit 'We Can't Stop'.

6

The 1976 single 'Music' was the first of two Top 10 hits for John Miles – what was the other?

7

Although different songs, what title is shared between hit singles by Whitney Houston in 1996, New Kids on the Block in 1990 and Joe Simon in 1973?

8

What was the title of the only single by Mike and the Mechanics to make the Top 10?

9

Name the Welsh-born singer who sang about a 'Crazy Chick' on her 2005 Top 3 single.

10

Which of these three Top 40 hits by Sparks gained the highest chart placing: 'Something for the Girl with Everything', 'Looks, Looks, Looks' or 'Beat the Clock'?

TOP **50**

QUIZ **21**

Which musician had a Top 5 hit with the theme music to the TV series *Miami Vice*?

Which band's first two Top 5 hits of the 1970s were 'All Right Now' and 'My Brother Jake'?

Released in 1977, what was the title of the debut hit and first Top 10 single achieved by Chic?

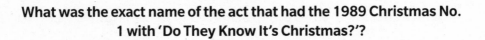

What was the exact name of the act that had the 1989 Christmas No. 1 with 'Do They Know It's Christmas?'?

Who was the featured singer on Clean Bandit's 2014 No. 1, 'Rather Be'?

'Pass the Dutchie' was a 1982 No. 1 hit for which UK reggae group?

What was the title of the 1980 album by John Lennon and Yoko Ono that became a posthumous No. 1 for the former Beatle in 1981?

Which other act joined Diana Ross and the Supremes on the 1969 Top 3 single 'I'm Gonna Make You Love Me'?

Name either of the two Top 10 singles achieved by Swing Out Sister in the 1980s.

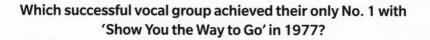

Which successful vocal group achieved their only No. 1 with 'Show You the Way to Go' in 1977?

QUIZ **22**

1

With which hit-making band do you associate the late Phil Lynott?

2

Who had Top 10 hits in the early 1960s with 'If She Should Come to You' and 'Strawberry Fair'?

3

Which hit song from *Grease* did Hylda Baker and Arthur Mullard take back into the Top 40 in 1978?

4

What was the title of the song that gave Unit Four Plus Two their 1965 No. 1 hit?

5

Which female singer topped the album charts in 1995 with her LP *Daydream*?

6

Which of these three Oasis singles from 2000 was the only one to reach No. 1: 'Who Feels Love?', 'Sunday Morning Call' or 'Go Let It Out'?

7

'Vienna' and 'Dancing with Tears in My Eyes' were the two biggest hits for which successful group?

8

Who, in 2018, released the No. 1 album *Staying at Tamara's*?

(9)

Which 2005 Top 10 single by Girls Aloud shares the same three-word title as a 1983 Top 10 song by the Style Council?

(10)

What is the title of the 1965 debut No. 1 hit by the Righteous Brothers?

TOP **50**

QUIZ **23**

(((1)))

With which 1980s No. 1 group do you associate Eddi Reader?

(((2)))

What was the title of Dusty Springfield's 1970 Top 40 hit that would become a No. 1 for David Cassidy two years later?

(((3)))

Which Top 3 hit from 1982 by Yazoo did the Flying Pickets take to No. 1 the following year?

(((4)))

What was the title of M People's 1993 Top 3 hit, which was included in the movies *The First Wives Club* and *The Full Monty*?

(((5)))

Which successful 1960s singer had a backing group named the Pirates?

(((6)))

'My Perfect Cousin' was the only Top 10 hit for which band from Northern Ireland?

(((7)))

Which female singer entered the charts at No. 1 at the end of 2006 with her single 'A Moment Like This'?

(((8)))

The 1976 Top 10 single '(Do the) Spanish Hustle' was a hit for which group?

9

Ranking Ann was featured on the 1985 Top 10 single 'The Word Girl' recorded by which group?

10

In 2002, Ronan Keating had a Top 5 hit duet with Lulu – what was the title?

QUIZ **24**

Who duetted with Cliff Richard on the 1983 Top 10 single, 'She Means Nothing to Me'?

The vocal group En Vogue had four Top 10 singles in the 1990s – three in their own right and one with Salt-N-Pepa: name any two of these four.

Name the duo who first topped the album charts in 1968 with *Bookends*.

From 1961, what was the title of John Leyton's only No. 1 hit?

The song 'That's My Goal' became the No. 1 chart debut at the end of 2005 for which singer?

The group Imagination first reached the charts in 1981 with which Top 5 song?

Name the group formed by Jimmy Somerville after his departure from Bronski Beat.

'Should I Stay or Should I Go' was a belated No. 1 in 1991 for which punk band?

Can you name the act that reached No. 1 in 1980 with their hit 'Use It Up and Wear It Out'?

Two chart acts have had different Top 10 singles this century called 'Issues' – a girl group in 2009 and a solo female vocalist in 2017. Name either of these acts.

ANSWERS QUIZ 23

1. Fairground Attraction 2. 'How Can I Be Sure' 3. 'Only You', 4. 'Moving On Up', 5. Johnny Kidd 6. The Undertones 7. Leona Lewis 8. The Fatback Band 9. Scritti Politti 10. 'We've Got Tonight'

QUIZ **25**

1

Which brother and sister duo had hits with the songs 'Top of the World', 'Only Yesterday' and 'I Won't Last a Day Without You'?

2

What question did R.E.M. ask 'Kenneth' according to the title of the group's 1994 Top 10 single?

3

In 2016, which Tracy Chapman hit from 1988 was successfully revived by Jonas Blue & Dakota?

4

What is the name of the former *EastEnders*' actor who had a Top 20 hit in 2000 with 'Good Thing Going'?

5

Which U2 song was a Top 10 single for the Chimes in 1990?

6

What was the name of the musical in which David Essex's 1978 Top 10 hit 'Oh What a Circus' was featured?

7

What was the name of the group that made the Top 20 in the 1960s with 'Friday on My Mind' and 'Hello, How Are You'?

8

Who duetted with Bill Medley on the Top 10 hit in both 1987 and 1991, '(I've Had) The Time of My Life', as featured in the movie *Dirty Dancing*?

9

The song 'Apeman' was Top 5 hit in the early 1970s for which group?

10

In 1995, which legendary pop group returned to the Top 10 for the first time since 1982 with their single 'Baby It's You'?

TOP **50**

QUIZ **26**

In which year did Elaine Paige and Barbara Dickson spend a month at No. 1 with 'I Know Him So Well'?

What was the title of Rick Astley's debut No. 1 hit?

What was the title of the Joni Mitchell hit in which she mentioned a 'pink hotel'?

Released towards the end of 1998, which pop vocal group reached No. 1 early in 1999 with the songs 'Heartbeat' and 'Tragedy', a cover of the Bee Gees' No. 1 from 1979?

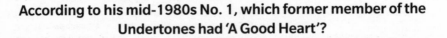

According to his mid-1980s No. 1, which former member of the Undertones had 'A Good Heart'?

The 2011 *X Factor* finalists reached No. 1 with a cover of which Rose Royce song?

What are the first names of the Fogerty brothers in Creedence Clearwater Revival?

What 2003 Top 3 single by Justin Timberlake shares the same title as the one and only chart hit from 1957 for the singer Julie London?

Released in 1985, what is the title of the only single by Stephen 'Tin Tin' Duffy to make the Top 10?

What is the title of the only single by Stephen 'Tin Tin' Duffy to make the Top 10?

Name the singer who joined Kim Wilde on her 1987 Top 10 hit 'Another Step (Closer to You)'.

QUIZ **27**

1

'The Look' and 'Joyride' were Top 10 hits for which Swedish duo?

2

Who was the bass player in the classic line-up of Queen?

3

Marianne Faithfull had a Top 40 hit in 1965 with her version of which Lennon & McCartney song?

4

Name the group that made the Top 10 with their hits 'Public Image' and 'This Is Not a Love Song'.

5

In which successful Motown act was Eddie Kendricks once a member?

6

In 2002, a single by Nelly featuring Kelly Rowland spent two weeks at No. 1 – what is it called?

7

Which reggae band topped the album charts for 12 consecutive weeks in 1984 with their 'best of' album called *Legend*?

8

In which year did the TV music show *The Old Grey Whistle Test* first air?

In 1979, who joined Donna Summer on the Top 3 duet 'No More Tears (Enough Is Enough)'?

Which famous actor joined Sharleen Spiteri in the video to the Texas song 'In Demand'?

TOP **50**

ANSWERS QUIZ 26

1. 1985 2. 'Never Gonna Give You Up' 3. 'Big Yellow Taxi' 4. Steps 5. Feargal Sharkey 6. 'Wishing on a Star' 7. John and Tom 8. 'Cry Me a River' 9. 'Kiss Me' 10. Junior

QUIZ **28**

1

First released in 1961, which one-time singer with the Drifters had a No. 1 hit in 1987 with 'Stand By Me'?

2

Name the band that released the No. 1 albums *Parachutes* and *A Rush of Blood to the Head*.

3

What is the title of the 1985 Top 20 single recorded by David Bowie with the Pat Metheny Group?

4

Scoring most of his hits in the 1960s, by what name was singer Ronald Wycherley better known?

5

What was the title of the 1988 debut Top 10 hit by Inner City that featured Kevin Saunderson?

Who joined UB40 on their 1990 Top 10 hit 'I'll Be Your Baby Tonight'?

Roy Orbison had a posthumous duet in 1992 with Canadian singer k. d. lang – what is it called?

'There It Is' and 'A Night to Remember' were Top 5 hits in 1982 for which successful group?

The band Chicago had their only UK No. 1 in 1976 – what was it called?

Which singer starred in the 1980s movie, *Who's That Girl?*

ANSWERS QUIZ **27**

1. Roxette 2. John Deacon 3. 'Yesterday' 4. Public Image Ltd 5. The Temptations 6. 'Dilemma' 7. Bob Marley & the Wailers 8. 1971 9. Barbra Streisand 10. Alan Rickman

QUIZ **29**

1

According to their 1984 Top 3 hit, who claimed 'It's Raining Men'?

2

With which musical instrument do you associate Cozy Powell?

3

What girl's name that was the subject of hits by both Little Richard and Kenny Rogers?

4

Which legendary singer once lived in a mansion in Memphis called Graceland?

5

What is the title of Dizzee Rascal's 2013 Top 5 single that features Robbie Williams?

6

Name the act that had a Top 3 hit in 1961 with 'Are You Sure' – the UK's Eurovision entry that year.

7

Ian Hunter of Mott the Hoople had his only Top 40 solo hit in 1975 with which song?

8

With which successful band do you associate Chrissie Hynde?

Which successful chart artist of the 1980s wrote Chesney Hawkes's 1991 No. 1 'The One and Only'?

Name the performer who topped the charts in 1996 with 'Return of the Mack'.

TOP **50**

ANSWERS QUIZ **28**

10. Madonna
1. Ben E. King 2. Coldplay 3. 'This Is Not America' 4. Billy Fury 5. 'Big Fun' 6. Robert Palmer 7. 'Crying' 8. Shalamar 9. 'If You Leave Me Now'

QUIZ **30**

1

Who sang with Nancy Sinatra on her 1967 Top 20 hit 'Jackson'?

2

Which Crowded House song became a Top 20 cover in 1991 for Paul Young?

3

'How Do You Sleep?' was a Top 10 single in 2019 for which singer?

4

Which '... Park' was visited by the Small Faces in both 1967 and 1975?

5

Which Stevie Wonder song became a Top 5 hit in 1999 for George Michael and Mary J. Blige?

6

The late 1980s single 'Beds Are Burning' was the only Top 10 hit for which Australian band?

7

What was the title of actor Telly Savalas's 1975 No. 1?

8

Name the band that had No. 1 albums in the 2000s with *Amnesiac*, *Hail to the Thief* and *In Rainbows*.

9

What was the name of Georgie Fame's backing group featured on some of his earlier hits?

10

Which country singer wrote Whitney Houston's 1992 No. 1 'I Will Always Love You'?

QUIZ **31**

Which song title gave major hits in the 1980s to Huey Lewis and the News, Jennifer Rush and Frankie Goes to Hollywood?

In 1981, which act sang about 'Joan of Arc'?

According to the Beatles 1965 American No. 1 hit, how many days are there in a week?

In which Elton John hit from 1974 does he sing 'Goodbye' to Norma Jean?

Which female singer had a hit both in 1962 and 1972 with 'The Loco-Motion'?

Name the duo who topped the album charts in 1993 with *Very*.

Which actress and singer is known as 'The Divine Miss M'?

In 1999, Madness had their first Top 10 hit since 1992 – what was the title?

Name the other four members of Dave Dee's hit-making group of the 1960s.

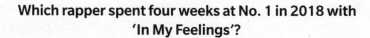

Which rapper spent four weeks at No. 1 in 2018 with 'In My Feelings'?

QUIZ **32**

1

'Glass of Champagne' and 'Girls Girls Girls' were Top 10 singles for which 1970s group?

2

What was the title of the only No. 1 the Tremeloes achieved with Brian Poole as their lead singer?

3

Name the act that topped the charts in 1982 with 'The Lion Sleeps Tonight'.

4

In 1977, which singer and songwriter claimed in her Top 10 hit that 'You're Moving Out Today'?

5

What is the title of the 2018 No. 1 by Clean Bandit that features Demi Lovato as guest vocalist?

6

Which two Motown acts joined forces in 1971 to successfully revive Ike and Tina Turner's 1966 hit, 'River Deep – Mountain High'?

7

The song 'Mary's Prayer' was a Top 3 single in the spring of 1988 for which chart act?

8

Who had No. 1 albums in the mid-1970s with *Smiler*, *Atlantic Crossing* and *A Night on the Town*?

9

Before pursuing a solo career, Darren Hayes was the lead singer with which successful duo?

10

'Damn I Wish I Was Your Lover' and 'Right Beside You' were the only two Top 20 hits for which American singer-songwriter?

TOP **50**

QUIZ **33**

What was the name of the hotel where the Eagles stayed according to the band's 1976 album and 1977 single?

The 1993 Top 20 hit 'A Whole New World' by Peabo Bryson and Regina Belle featured in which Disney movie?

Which 1960s instrumental group had Top 10 hits with 'Guitar Tango' and 'Shindig'?

What 1970 Top 10 single by the Temptations has the subtitle '(That's What the World Is Today)'?

According to their 1991 Top 20 hit, which group were 'Losing My Religion'?

What did Toyah 'Want to Be ...' according to the title of her 1981 Top 10 song?

Which brothers had Top 20 hits in the 1970s with 'Summer Breeze' and 'It's a Disco Night (Rock Don't Stop)'?

'Shallow' was a 2018 No. 1 hit for Lady Gaga and which other performer?

(((9)))

Actor Vincent Price provided the chilling spoken voice on which 1983 Top 10 hit?

(((10)))

What was the name of Billy J. Kramer's backing group?

QUIZ **34**

1

Name the singer who partnered Dave Stewart in Eurythmics.

2

Which Irish group had their debut hit in 1988 with 'Don't Go' – a song they performed during the interval at the Eurovision Song Contest in Dublin that year?

3

Which country singer and songwriter co-wrote Olivia Newton-John's 1973 Top 20 hit, 'Take Me Home Country Roads'?

4

What was the title of the only solo single by John Travolta to make the Top 10?

5

According to his 2016 No. 1 hit, who 'Took a Pill in Ibiza'?

6

In 1991, Queen topped the charts with a double 'A' sided hit, a reissue of 'Bohemian Rhapsody' and which other song?

7

Which actor and singer made the Top 10 in second half of the 1970s with his hits 'Dancing with the Captain' and 'Grandma's Party'?

Name the legendary rock band that made their Top 10 chart debut in 1968 with 'Pictures of Matchstick Men'.

Aja **was the title of the only Top 10 studio album for which American band?**

Which member of the Sex Pistols went on to form Public Image Ltd?

TOP **50**

QUIZ **35**

Name the Canadian singer and guitarist who made his UK chart debut in 1985 with the song 'Run to You'.

Which American group had Top 5 hits in 1979 with 'I Want Your Love' and 'Good Times'?

Released in 1968, the Move had their only No. 1 single in February 1969 with which song?

The Canadian dance duo of Rosalind Hunt and Lyn Cullerier made their only UK chart appearance in 1982 with a song called 'Murphy's Law' – under what name did they record this?

The singer Conner Reeves had all four of his solo Top 40 hits in 1997–8 – name one of them.

Who spent four weeks at No. 1 in 2015 with the Felix Jaehn remix of 'Cheerleader'?

Which group first made the Top 10 in 1998 with 'Mulder and Scully'?

What was the title of Perry Como's only Top 10 hit of the 1960s?

Who had Top 10 albums in the 1970s with *Journey Through the Secret Life of Plants* and *Songs in the Key of Life*?

What was the title of the Top 5 song with which Milk and Honey featuring Gali Atari won the Eurovision Song Contest in 1979?

QUIZ **36**

1

In 1980, which UK disco group suggested you 'Dance Yourself Dizzy'?

2

Which group's hits in the 1960s included 'Happy Jack', 'Magic Bus' and 'Anyway Anyhow Anywhere'?

3

The 1982 song 'Da Da Da' was the only hit single for which German three-piece?

4

What was the title of the 1987 debut Top 10 hit for Living in a Box?

5

What is the title of the 1990 solo chart debut by Jon Bon Jovi associated with the Emilio Estevez film *Young Guns II*?

6

'Jungle Rock', a track recorded in the late 1950s, became a Top 3 hit in 1976 for which American singer and guitarist?

7

Which legendary soul singer was featured on the Eurythmics' 1985 Top 10 single 'Sisters Are Doing It for Themselves'?

In 1962, Elvis Presley topped the chart with his double 'A' sided hit 'Rock-A-Hula Baby' and which other song?

'Love Rears Its Ugly Head' was the only UK Top 20 hit for which American rock band?

Although different songs, what hit title is shared by Modern Talking and Hot Chocolate?

TOP **50**

QUIZ 37

(((1)))

In 1979, Pink Floyd topped the singles chart for the only time with which song?

(((2)))

'Bus Stop' and 'Stop Stop Stop' were Top 5 hits in 1966 for which successful group?

(((3)))

From 1992, what was the title of the only No. 1 hit for Boyz II Men?

(((4)))

Name the classical guitarist who made the Top 20 in 1979 with his instrumental 'Cavatina'.

(((5)))

Which group had Top 10 albums in the 1960s with *Smiley Smile* and *Wild Honey*?

(((6)))

In 1972, Wings made the Top 10 with a song that shared its title with which children's nursery rhyme?

(((7)))

Who sang about 'Budapest' on his hit that reached the Top 5 in 2014?

(((8)))

Name either of the two Top 10 singles by Transvision Vamp during the late 1980s.

9

What is the name of the American female singer who was backed by the Vandellas?

10

From which musical was the hit duet 'All I Ask of You' by Cliff Richard and Sarah Brightman taken?

QUIZ **38**

In 1965, which female singer found herself in 'In the Middle of Nowhere'?

What was the title of the 1981 No. 1 hit by Roxy Music that was a tribute to John Lennon?

What is the name of the songwriting duo in Squeeze?

Name the group whose No. 1 albums included *Arrival* and *The Visitors*.

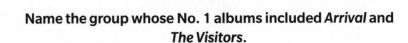

What is the title of Bruce Springsteen's 1994 Top 3 award-winning song for a film starring Tom Hanks, Denzel Washington and Antonio Banderas?

Norwegian producer Kygo is billed alongside Whitney Houston on which posthumous 2019 Top 3 song?

Which hit-making guitarist had a backing group called the Rebels?

Prior to joining AC/DC, Brian Johnson sang lead vocals with a band that had hits in 1973 with 'All Because of You' and 'Can You Do It' – what were they called?

Sigue Sigue Sputnik had their only Top 10 single in 1986 – what is it called?

Name the instrumental group that had Top 10 hits in the early 1960s with 'Walk Don't Run' and 'Perfidia'.

ANSWERS QUIZ 37

1. 'Another Brick in the Wall (Part 2)' 2. The Hollies 3. 'End of the Road' 4. John Williams 5. The Beach Boys 6. 'Mary Had a Little Lamb' 7. George Ezra 8. 'I Want Your Love' (No. 5 in 1988), 'Baby I Don't Care' (No. 3 in 1989) 9. Martha Reeves 10. *The Phantom of the Opera*

QUIZ 39

1

'Take Good Care of My Baby' and 'Run to Him' were Top 10 hits in the early 1960s for which American singer?

2

What was the title of 1986 Feargal Sharkey's Top 5 follow-up to his 1985 No. 1 'A Good Heart'?

3

According to her 2019 Top 5 hit, which singer said 'You Need to Calm Down'?

4

Limmie and the Family Cookin' achieved two Top 10 hits during the 1970s – one was 'You Can Do Magic' but what was the other?

5

What was the title of the only Top 10 hit achieved by Alison Limerick in 1996 – a remix of her Top 40 debut in 1991?

6

Name the group that, in the late 1970s, had hit covers of the American 1960s hits 'Duke of Earl' by Gene Chandler (as lead singer of the Dukays) and 'Boy from New York City' by the Ad Libs.

7

'You Can Call Me Al' was one of two Top 40 hits from Paul Simon's No. 1 album *Graceland* – what was the other?

8

What was the title of DNA's Top 3 hit from 1990 that featured Suzanne Vega?

9

'If I Said You Had a Beautiful Body Would You Hold It Against Me' was a 1979 Top 10 hit for which American act?

10

Which rock band had Top 5 albums in the 1980s with the titles *Eliminator* and *Afterburner*?

TOP **50**

QUIZ **40**

Which band had hits in the early 1980s with the songs 'Mirror in the Bathroom', 'Best Friend' and 'Hand's Off ... She's Mine'?

Who wrote Rod Stewart's 1993 Top 5 hit, 'Have I Told You Lately'?

What was the title of the 2003 Top 3 hit recorded by Craig David and Sting?

In 1965, 'Message Understood' and 'I'll Stop at Nothing' were both Top 10 hits for which female singer?

In 1979, which singer topped the charts with her one and only hit, 'Ring My Bell'?

Which member of the Spice Girls sang the 1998 Top 3 song 'When You're Gone' with Bryan Adams?

Mike McGear, John Gorman and Roger McGough were all members of which successful act from the 1960s and 1970s?

In 1988, Heart achieved a double 'A' sided Top 10 hit with 'Never' and which other song?

Which boyband had No. 1 albums in the 1990s with *Said and Done*, *A Different Beat* and *Where We Belong*?

The song 'Walk Away from Love' was a Top 10 hit in 1976 for a former member of the Temptations – who was he?

ANSWERS QUIZ **39**

QUIZ **41**

1

Which male singer's first two Top 10 hits came in 1964 with 'Hold Me' and 'Together'?

2

Who were credited for writing Wet Wet Wet's 1988 No. 1 hit, 'With a Little Help from My Friends'?

3

What was the title of the 2005 No. 1 by 2Pac featuring Elton John?

4

The singer Melanie had all four of her Top 40 hits in the early 1970s, beginning with 'Ruby Tuesday' in 1970 and ending with 'Will You Still Love Me Tomorrow' in 1974 – name one of the two in between.

5

'Robert De Niro' was claimed to be waiting for which girl group in 1984?

6

What was the title of Procol Harum's Top 10 follow-up to their 1967 No. 1 hit 'A Whiter Shade of Pale'?

7

In 2001, which boyband successfully brought Billy Joel's 1983 'Uptown Girl' back to No. 1?

Name the band that topped the album charts in the 1980s with *Love Over Gold* and in the 1990s with *On Every Street*.

Who did Phil Collins sing alongside on the 1985 No. 1 hit 'Easy Lover'?

Not counting hyphenated words, six of the Top 40 hits by Travis have one word titles – name any two of them.

ANSWERS QUIZ 40

1. The Beat 2. Van Morrison 3. 'Rise & Fall' 4. Sandie Shaw 5. Anita Ward 6. Melanie C 7. The Scaffold 8. 'These Dreams' 9. Boyzone 10. David Ruffin

QUIZ **42**

'Poison Arrow' and 'The Look of Love' were the first two singles to reach the Top 10 for which group?

Which Irish group made the Top 10 in 1982 with the theme to the TV series *Harry's Game*?

In which year did the Beatles make their chart debut with the song 'Love Me Do'?

Name the female singer who is featured on Quincy Jones's 1981 single 'Razzamatazz'.

Which act achieved the most No. 1 singles during the 1970s, Abba or Slade?

Emma Bunton had her only No. 1 as a solo artist in 2001 –
what is it called?

In 1978, which group dialled the numbers '5.7.0.5' all the
way into the Top 10?

Although different songs, what title is shared by Tom Jones
and Bobbie Gentry on hit singles in the 1960s?

Which successful group achieved No. 1 albums in the 1980s
with *The Hurting* and *The Seeds of Love*?

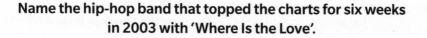

Name the hip-hop band that topped the charts for six weeks
in 2003 with 'Where Is the Love'.

QUIZ **43**

1

Who had her first Top 40 hit in 1964 with the Top 10 song 'Walk On By'?

2

'All the Young Dudes' was the first of three Top 10 singles for Mott the Hoople in the 1970s – can you name either of the other two?

3

Name the singer who topped the album charts in the 1990s with *The Colour of My Love* and *Falling into You*.

4

Otis Redding and Carla Thomas are credited as having two hit duets, both in 1967 – name either of them.

5

Name both the group and the singer who reached the Top 10 in 1984 with the song 'Ain't Nobody'.

6

As of 2020, the singer-songwriter Jack Savoretti has had three Top 10 albums – name one of these three releases.

7

Which group did 1960s prime minister Harold Wilson sue over the use of his image for the publicity of their record 'Flowers in the Rain'?

Name the musical that features Jennifer Holliday's 1982 Top 40 hit 'And I'm Telling You I'm Not Going'.

'Walk on the Wild Side' was a Top 10 hit in 1973 for which singer and songwriter?

Name both the actor who plays Paul Robinson in *Neighbours* and the title of his 1989 hit single – his only Top 40 appearance.

TOP **50**

QUIZ **44**

1

What month of the year gave Earth, Wind and Fire the title of their first UK Top 10 hit?

2

According to her 1985 Top 20 hit, who was in love with 'The Belle of St Mark'?

3

Which group had the most No. 1 hits during the 1990s, Take That or Boyzone?

4

The duo Mouth & MacNeal had a Top 10 hit in 1974 with the song that represented Holland in the 1974 Eurovision Song Contest – what is it called?

5

Who wrote the Monkees' 1967 No. 1 hit 'I'm a Believer'?

6

Which band had No. 1 albums in the 1990s with *Parklife* and *The Great Escape*?

7

The New Seekers made their final Top 40 appearance in 1978 with a song that has the subtitle '(One Day in Every Week)' – what is it called?

(((8)))

James Taylor's 1971 version of
Carole King's 'You've Got a Friend'
is his only Top 10 single, but which
group had their only Top 10 hit with
a version of that same song in 1997?

(((9)))

'Wrecking Ball' was a 2013 No. 1 hit
for which singer?

(((10)))

Who had Top 10 hits in the 1960s
with the ballads 'Softly as I Leave
You' and 'Walk Away'?

ANSWERS QUIZ **43**

1. Dionne Warwick 2. 'All the Way from Memphis', 'Roll Away the Stone'
3. Céline Dion 4. 'Tramp', 'Knock On Wood' 5. Rufus and Chaka Khan
6. *Written in Scars* (2015), reached Top 10 in 2016), *Sleep No More* (2016),
Singing to Strangers (2019, No. 1) 7. The Move 8. *Dreamgirls* 9. Lou Reed
10. Stefan Dennis, 'Don't it Make You Feel Good'

QUIZ **45**

Who sang with the Sutherland Brothers on their 1976 Top 5 hit 'Arms of Mary'?

Who wrote 'Here Comes My Baby', the Tremeloes' first hit without Brian Poole?

From 1986, what is the title of the only solo Top 10 hit for Deborah Harry?

In 1991, which singer made the Top 20 with her cover of Elton John's 'Rocket Man (I Think It's Gonna Be a Long, Long Time)'?

Who topped the album charts during the 1970s with *Tubular Bells* and *Hergest Ridge*?

6

What were the first names of brother and sister act the Carpenters?

7

Which vocal group is featured alongside B*Witched on the 1999 Top 20 song 'I Shall Be There'?

8

Name the only No. 1 hit for Spandau Ballet.

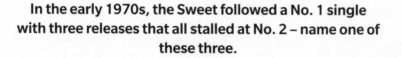

9

In the early 1970s, the Sweet followed a No. 1 single with three releases that all stalled at No. 2 – name one of these three.

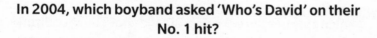

10

In 2004, which boyband asked 'Who's David' on their No. 1 hit?

ANSWERS QUIZ **44**

1. September 2. Sheila E 3. Take That (eight), Boyzone (six) (Take That have had four further No. 1s since reforming in 2006) 4. 'I See a Star' 5. Neil Diamond 6. Blur 7. 'Anthem' 8. The Brand New Heavies 9. Miley Cyrus 10. Matt Monro

QUIZ **46**

1

'The Stonk' was a No. 1 single in 1991 for which comedy double act?

2

Rod Stewart is the uncredited vocalist on a 1972 Top 3 single by Python Lee Jackson – what was the song called?

3

Which singer reached No. 1 in 1987 with his version of 'Everything I Own'?

4

Although different songs, what title is shared by Top 10 hits for David Essex in 1982 and Queen in 1995?

5

In 2008, who joined Madonna on the No. 1 hit '4 Minutes'?

6

Dave and Ansel Collins topped the charts with 'Double Barrel' in 1971, but what was the title of their Top 10 follow-up hit?

7

According to her 1999 No. 1, which singer kept her 'Genie in a Bottle'?

8

Complete the title from this 1988 Top 3 song by Billy Ocean: 'Get Outta My Dreams, ...'.

9

From 1975, name the only Top 10 hit for the group Jigsaw.

10

In 1968, who was peddling up the charts on 'Les Bicyclettes de Belsize'?

TOP **50**

ANSWERS QUIZ **45**

1. Quiver 2. Cat Stevens 3. 'French Kissin' in the USA' 4. Kate Bush 5. Mike Oldfield 6. Richard and Karen 7. Ladysmith Black Mambazo 8. 'True' 9. 'Hell Raiser', 'The Ballroom Blitz' (both 1973), 'Teenage Rampage' (1974) 10. Busted

QUIZ **47**

Complete this song title from a 1983 Top 10 hit by the Police, 'Wrapped Around ...'

Name the singer who made the Top 10 in 1971 with 'Something Tells Me (Something's Gonna Happen Tonight)'.

Who joined Julio Iglesias on the 1984 Top 20 song 'To All the Girls I've Loved Before'?

Who were XTC 'Making Plans for ...' according to the group's first Top 40 single in 1979?

Which singer's highest charting single came in 1995 with her Top 5 hit 'It's Oh So Quiet'?

According to their 1969 Top 3 hit, which band was 'Living in the Past'?

What is the title of the 1987 Top 3 song by Pet Shop Boys featuring Dusty Springfield?

In 2005, which group said, 'I Bet You Look Good on the Dancefloor'?

Name the Irish singer who successfully covered Bob Lind's 1966 Top 5 hit 'Elusive Butterfly' in the same year.

Apparently, Westlife achieved the impossible on their 1999 No. 1 by 'Flying Without ...' who or what?

QUIZ **48**

1

In 1975, which 'flighty' group were 'Walking in Rhythm'?

2

Who had Top 10 albums in the 1980s with *The Dream of the Blue Turtles* and *Nothing Like the Sun*?

3

'Mysterious Girl' was a Top 5 hit both in 1996 and again in 2004 when it topped the charts for which singer?

4

Which comedy act joined Cliff Richard on a 1986 revival of his first No. 1, 'Living Doll'?

5

What is the French title of the 1997 Top 3 chart debut for Sash!?

6

Which movie featured the 1962 No. 1 hit 'Moon River' by Danny Williams?

7

Who sang about her 'Milkshake' on her single that spent a month at No. 2 in 2004?

8

Brian May achieved two solo Top 10 hits during the early 1990s. The first was 'Driven by You' but what was the title of the other?

9

In 1975, which rock band said 'Roll Over Lay Down'?

10

Which act had the most No. 1 hits during the 1980s, Bucks Fizz or the Bee Gees?

TOP **50**

ANSWERS QUIZ **47**

1. '... Your Finger' 2. Cilla Black (also the theme song to her TV series at the time) 3. Willie Nelson 4. '... Nigel' 5. Björk 6. Jethro Tull 7. 'What Have I Done to Deserve This?' 8. The Arctic Monkeys 9. Val Doonican (the two versions were in the Top 10 at the same time) 10. '... Wings'

QUIZ **49**

In 1971, who said 'He's Gonna Step on You Again' on his Top 5 single?

Name the singer who was featured on West End's 1993 Top 3 hit, 'The Love I Lost'.

Which 1960s group became the first to achieve three consecutive Christmas No. 1 hits?

Which girl group entered the charts at No. 1 in 2005 with 'Push the Button'?

Name the successful band that topped the album charts in the 1970s with *Sticky Fingers* and *Exile on Main Street*.

From 1979, what was the title of the only Top 10 hit achieved by Lene Lovich?

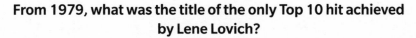

What type of '... Girl' did Tori Amos sing about on her 1994 Top 5 song?

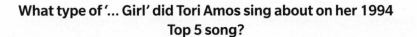

Who is the name of the uncredited female singer who featured on Meat Loaf's 1981 single 'Dead Ringer for Love'?

Counting double 'A' sides as one, who had the most No. 1s in the 1990s, S Club 7 or All Saints?

In 1973, which female singer suffered the '48 Crash'?

ANSWERS QUIZ **48**

1. The Blackbyrds 2. Sting 3. Peter Andre (full credit for 1996 release: Peter Andre featuring Bubbler Ranx) 4. The Young Ones 5. 'Encore une Fois' 6. *Breakfast at Tiffany's* ('Moon River' entered the charts in November 1961 and became the first new No. 1 of 1962) 7. Kelis 8. 'Too Much Love Will Kill You' 9. Status Quo 10. Bucks Fizz (three), the Bee Gees (one)

QUIZ **50**

By what name is singer and songwriter Robert Zimmerman better known?

Jimmy Cliff had just two Top 10 singles during his chart career – one in 1969, the other in 1970 – and both have the word 'World' their titles. Name both songs.

The title of track of a-ha's 1985 Top 3 debut album was a Top 5 single for the group in 1986 – what is the title of that album and single?

Mr Wonderful in the 1960s, *Mirage* in the 1980s and *Say You Will* in the 2000s have all been Top 10 studio albums for which group?

Including collaborations (but not including Wham! or Band Aid), who had the most No. 1 hits during the 1980s, George Michael or Shakin' Stevens?

What is the title of the 2011 Top 10 chart debut by Lana Del Rey?

Which group had Top 10 hits in the 1970s with 'There's a Whole Lot of Loving' and 'You Don't Have to Say You Love Me'?

The American group Atlantic Starr had two Top 10 singles in the 1980s – name both of them.

'Pamela' was the last solo hit of the 1960s for which singer?

In 1987, which legendary group joined the Fat Boys on their Top 3 hit 'Wipeout'?

TOP **50**

Hopefully you've survived and enjoyed the 50 sets of questions in the previous section. So now we move on to the Top 40 – 40 sets of questions split into 4 categories.

To begin, in quizzes 1–10, we'll be going through the decades from the 1950s to the 2010s, with double 'A' sides (which means two sets of questions!) for the 1970s, 1980s and 1990s.

After this, in quizzes 11–20, there's a whole group of questions on UK No. 1 singles – you'll need to find both the chart act and the song title to answer the clues.

Things then get mixed up a bit in quizzes 21–30 with 'Trio of Words'. One of the three names/words in the title will feature in the question or answer – or maybe both.

Finally, the Top 40 is rounded off with your chance to earn extra points – some classic albums from across the decades. There are ten clues each to ten albums, and you'll need to be honest with your own point scoring. If you can guess both the artist and album from the first clue (and very good luck with that!), award yourself 10 points. For each extra clue you need, deduct 1 point. So, if you need all ten clues, then your score is just 1.

QUIZ **1**

From 1957, what was the first hit and No. 1 achieved in the UK by the Crickets?

According to her 1954 No. 1 song, who claimed 'Little Things Mean a Lot'?

Two singers topped the charts in 1957 with 'Singing the Blues': one was Guy Mitchell, but who was the other?

Originally intended as the 'B' side, what was the title of Cliff Richard's first hit single that made the charts in 1958?

Which female singer made the Top 10 with her hits 'Someone Else's Roses' and 'If I Give My Heart to You'?

Which rock and roller had his last hit of the 1950s with 'Lovin' Up a Storm'?

Who duetted with Bing Crosby on the 1956 Top 10 hit 'True Love' from the movie *High Society*?

In 1957, who took a walk in 'The Garden of Eden' on his No. 1 hit?

Connie Francis topped the charts in 1958 with a double 'A' sided hit – one song was 'Carolina Moon', but what was the other?

Can you name the vocal group that reached No. 1 in 1955 with 'Hernando's Hideaway'?

ANSWERS QUIZ 50

1. Bob Dylan 2. 'Wonderful World, Beautiful People' (1969), 'Wild World' (1970) 3. 'Hunting High and Low' 4. Fleetwood Mac 5. Shakin' Stevens (four), George Michael (three) 6. 'Video Games' 7. Guys and Dolls/Guys 'n' Dolls 8. 'Secret Lovers' (1986), 'Always' (1987) 9. Wayne Fontana 1 0. The Beach Boys

QUIZ **2**

Hits of the 1960s

1

Which actor-singer made his final appearance in the Top 40 in 1963 with 'I'll Cut Your Tail Off'?

2

Can you name the group whose only Top 40 hit was their 1968 release 'Smokey Blues Away'?

3

Which Lennon & McCartney song was both a Top 20 for St Louis Union and Top 30 hit for the Truth in 1966?

4

Which female singer made the Top 40 in the early 1960s with 'The Big Hurt' and 'Like I Do'?

5

How many No. 1 hits were achieved by guitarist Duane Eddy during the 1960s?

6

The 1968 singles 'Valleri' and 'D. W. Washburn' were the final two Top 40 hits of the 1960s for which TV manufactured group?

7

Both of the 1963 hit singles by the Chiffons have the word 'Fine' somewhere in the title – name both of them.

8

Name the singer who reached No. 2 in 1969 with his only solo hit of the decade, 'Saved by the Bell'.

9

'Stranger on the Shore' was a Top 3 instrumental hit for Acker Bilk in January 1962, but which American easy-listening singer had a Top 30 hit with a vocal version of that tune in the summer of that same year?

10

Which orchestra leader topped the charts in 1968 with the theme from the movie *The Good, the Bad and the Ugly*?

TOP **40**

QUIZ **3**

What was the title of the 1976 Top 5 debut hit for the American vocal group Tavares?

... and which American vocal group had both of their UK Top 40 hits in 1973 with the songs 'Armed and Extremely Dangerous' and 'Smarty Pants'?

Placed second in the 1970 Eurovision Song Contest, who sang the UK entry 'Knock, Knock Who's There?'?

Which legendary band made the Top 20 in the 1970s with 'Join Together', '5:15' and 'Let's See Action'?

The actor and singer Brian Protheroe made had his only hit single in 1974 with which song?

Can you name the singer who successfully revived Unit Four Plus Two's 1965 No. 1, 'Concrete and Clay', in 1976?

Sid Vicious was lead singer on two Top 3 hits for the Sex Pistols in 1979 that were covers of hits in the late 1950s for Eddie Cochran – name both these songs.

What was the title of the only UK Top 40 hit achieved by the American band Ides of March?

Who was the lead singer on the Rubettes' 1974 No. 1 hit, 'Sugar Baby Love'?

The singer who is the answer to the question above had his own Top 20 solo hit in the summer of that same year – what was it called?

ANSWERS QUIZ 2

0. Hugo Montenegro

6. The Monkees 7. 'He's So Fine', 'One Fine Day', 8. Robin Gibb 9. Andy Williams 1

1. John Leyton 2. New Generation 3. 'Girl' 4. Maureen Evans 5. None (his highest charting singles were 'Because They're Young' (1960) and 'Pepe' (1961), both of which stalled at No. 2)

QUIZ **4**

Hits of the 1970s ('AA')

1

Which band had both of their Top 40 hits in 1978 with the Top 5 song 'Airport' and the Top 20 hit 'Forget About You'?

2

Elvis Presley topped the charts twice in the 1970s, the second time with 'Way Down' in 1977, but what was the title of the first in 1970?

3

Which American chart act made its only UK appearance in 1977 with 'Spanish Stroll'?

4

Prior to Top 10 success in 1983 with 'Rockit', Herbie Hancock had two Top 20 singles in the late 1970s – name either of these.

5

The Tams spent three weeks at No. 1 in 1971 with which song, originally released in 1964?

6

In 1979, which legendary soul singer made the Top 10 with 'H.A.P.P.Y. Radio'?

7

'Judy Teen' was the title of the 1974 Top 10 chart debut by Cockney Rebel, but what was the title of the follow-up, also a Top 10 hit that year?

Which group achieved the first of 16 Top 40 hits in 1972 with 'Betcha by Golly Wow' and the last in 1977 with '$7000 and You?'

Of the total of five Top 40 singles for the Skids, two of them, both released in 1979, have one-word titles – name both of these singles.

Which Jamaican reggae singer achieved his only Top 20 hit in 1970 with 'Black Pearl'?

TOP **40**

QUIZ **5**

Who sang 'Wait' with Kym Mazelle on the 1989 Top 10 duet?

Go West's 1985 chart debut was also the duo's only Top 10 single, what is it called?

Which 1964 Doris Day Top 10 hit was successfully revived by Tracey Ullman in 1983?

Can you name the group whose only UK hit was the 1987 Top 3 hit 'Live It Up', featured in the movie *Crocodile Dundee*?

According to his 1980 Top 40 song, who claimed 'It's Hard to Be Humble'?

The new romantic group Landscape had both of their Top 40 singles in 1981 – 'Einstein a Go-Go' was the first, but who was the subject of the other?

What was the complete name of the act that made the Top 20 in 1985 with 'I Wonder If I Take You Home'?

The singer Maria Vidal made her only chart appearance in in the mid-1980s with a Top 20 single that was the theme song to a 1984 film about a young man with a talent for breakdancing – what is the song?

During the decade, the Thompson Twins had two Top 40 hits that included the word 'Doctor' or 'Dr' in the titles – name both of them.

How many No. 1 hits were achieved by Whitney Houston during the 1980s?

QUIZ **6**

1

'Build' was the final Top 20 hit of the 1980s for which band?

2

Name the group who had Top 10 albums in the 1980s with *Hysteria* and *Crash* and the No. 1 *Dare!*.

3

What were New Order 'Touched by ...' according to the title of their 1987 Top 20 single?

4

Who sang with Roberta Flack on the 1980 Top 10 duet 'Back Together Again'?

5

Name the Austrian group who achieved their only hit in 1985 with 'Live Is Life'.

6

Which rock band reached No. 9 on the charts in 1987 with their consecutive hits 'Is This Love' and the re-mix of 'Here I Go Again'?

7

What was the title of Boris Gardiner's 1986 No. 1 single?

8

Name the band whose 1980s hits included 'Something About You', 'Heaven in My Hands' and 'Hot Water'.

Which group revived the Chi-Lites 1974 Top 10 song 'Too Good to Be Forgotten' for a Top 5 hit in 1986?

During the 1980s Natalie Cole made the Top 10 on two occasions with her hits 'Miss You Like Crazy' and which other song (written by Bruce Springsteen)?

TOP **40**

QUIZ **7**

1

Led Zeppelin's only entry on the singles chart in the twentieth century came in 1997 with a song that had been a hit in America in 1969 – what is the song?

2

In 1997, which duo made the Top 3 with their version of the theme from the movie *The Saint*?

3

Which group featured alongside Tom Jones on his 1999 Top 10 hit 'Burning Down the House'?

4

In 1999, Martine McCutcheon made the Top 10 with her double 'A' sided cover versions of Yvonne Elliman's 'Love Me' and which other song?

5

Which 1967 Top 20 hit by the Turtles gave Jason Donovan a Top 10 cover version in 1991?

6

Under what name did Isaac Hayes reach No. 1 in the late 1990s with his hit 'Chocolate Salty Balls (PS I Love You)'?

7

Who reached the Top 10 in 1990 with her single '(We Want) The Same Thing'?

8

Can you name the act that made the Top 5 in 1992 with their hit 'Iron Lion Zion'?

9

Having amassed 21 Top 10 hits between 1968 and 1988, what was the title of the only Status Quo single to make the Top 10 during the 1990s?

10

Which other two performers joined Sting on their 1994 Top 3 hit 'All for Love', featured in the movie *The Three Musketeers*?

QUIZ **8**

Which two female singers along with Cher featured on the 1995 No. 1 hit 'Love Can Build a Bridge'?

What was the title of the first No. 1 hit single achieved by Blur?

Which group topped the charts for four weeks with 'Goodnight Girl' in 1992?

David Ball and Richard Norris had a Top 3 hit with 'Swamp Thing' in 1994 under what collective name?

In 1997, the Fun Lovin' Criminals made the Top 20 with the double 'A' sided hit that included a version of 10cc's 'I'm Not in Love' and what other song?

Calvin Cordozar Broadus Jr is the real name of which rapper who made his chart debut in 1993 with 'What's My Name?'?

Chris King, Winston Williams and Delroy St Joseph spent five weeks at No. 1 in 1992 with a dance version of KC & the Sunshine Band's 1979 hit 'Please Don't Go' under what collective name?

Elastica had three Top 40 hits in the mid-1990s – name both the group's lead singer and one of these three hits.

Name the singer who made the Top 3 in 1997 with the song 'Old Before I Die'.

According to the title of their 1994 Top 20 hit, where were Roxette 'Sleeping ...'?

ANSWERS QUIZ 7

1. 'Whole Lotta Love' (entered US charts November 1969, peaking at No. 4 early in 1970) 2. Orbital 3. The Cardigans 4. 'Talking in Your Sleep' (a hit for Crystal Gayle in 1978) 5. 'Happy Together' 6. Chef 7. Belinda Carlisle 8. Bob Marley & the Wailers 9. 'The Anniversary Waltz – Part 1' 10. Rod Stewart and Bryan Adams

QUIZ **9**

Who had Top 10 hits in 2004 with 'Irish Blood, English Heart' and 'Let Me Kiss You'?

Take That made a huge comeback in 2006 after being absent from the charts since 1996 – what was the title of their first comeback No. 1?

Which one-name female singer made the Top 20 in the year 2000 with her version of Cyndi Lauper's 1984 hit 'Girls Just Want to Have Fun'?

Name the rap and production duo who made the Top 10 in 2001 with 'Up Middle Finger'.

Which singer and guitarist had his only chart hit in 2001 with the Top 3 song with 'How Wonderful You Are'?

What was the title of the 2002 No. 1 hit by Blue that also featured Elton John?

In 2004, Atomic Kitten made the Top 10 with a double 'A' sided hit, 'Someone Like Me' and which other song?

Can you remember the title of the 1983 Top 3 song by Eddy Grant that returned to the Top 5 as a remix in 2001?

By what collective name were the duo Mark Brydon and Róisín Murphy better known?

The year 2008 was the most successful for the Ting Tings with four Top 40 singles beginning with the No. 1 'That's Not My Name' – name one of the other three.

TOP 40

ANSWERS QUIZ **8**

1. Neneh Cherry and Chrissie Hynde 2. 'Country House' 3. Wet Wet Wet 4. The Grid 5. 'Scooby Snacks' 6. Snoop Dogg (accept Snoop Doggy Dogg) 7. KWS (their surname initials: King, Williams, St Joseph) 8. Justine Frischmann; 'Line Up', 'Connection' (both 1994), 'Waking Up' (1995) 9. Robbie Williams 10. '… in My Car'

QUIZ **10**

Name the Paul Weller's Top 3 album from 2010 (his first album since 1982 to include the Jam's Bruce Foxton on bass) and the Top 40 song 'No Tears to Cry'.

Who was featured with Loud Luxury on the 2018 Top 10 hit 'Body'?

What was it 'Hotter Than …' according to the 2016 chart debut for Dua Lipa?

Name the band that entered the album charts at No. 1 in 2018 with *A Brief Enquiry into Online Relationships*.

What is the one-word title of the 2015 No. 1 by Years & Years?

Having had 17 Top 10 hits in the 2000s, name the female group whose only Top 10 hit in the 2010s was 'Wear My Kiss' in 2010?

The one-word title of a 2017 Top 20 single for the Script had previously provided different hit songs for Status Quo in the 1970s, the Cult in the 1980s and Madonna in the 1990s – what is that title?

In 2019, 'Bury a Friend' became the first Top 10 song for which American singer?

Under what name did the duo consisting of Jordan Stephens and Harley Alexander-Sule record their 2011 Top 10 hits 'Down with the Trumpets' and 'When I Was a Youngster'?

Name the singer who featured on Mick Ronson's 2018 Top 10 hit 'Nothing Breaks Like a Heart'?

ANSWERS QUIZ 9

1. Morrissey 2. 'Patience' 3. Lolly (her version is titled 'Girls Just Wanna Have Fun') 4. Oxide and Neutrino 5. Gordon Haskell 6. 'Sorry Seems to Be the Hardest Word' 7. 'Right Now 2004' (a remix of their debut hit for a 2004 Greatest Hits compilation) 8. 'Electric Avenue' 9. Moloko 10. 'Shut Up and Let Me Go', 'Great DJ', 'Be the One'

ULTIMATE POPMASTER 133

QUIZ **11**

For the next four quizzes, name both the No. 1 song and the chart act from the clues. Just to ease you into this section: some memory joggers from the decade of glam, teen idols and disco.

1

This became the first new No. 1 of the 1970s and the only record by this act to make the Top 40.

2

Reaching No. 1 in 1972, this song was adapted from a TV commercial for a famous soft drink.

3

A double 'A' side for this act in 1978 with one of the songs being 'Brown Girl in the Ring'.

4

The second of two No. 1 hit duets in 1978 from the movie *Grease*.

5

From 1974, the song was written by Johnny Bristol and was the only collective No. 1 for this family group.

6

The second of two No. 1 hits for this actor in 1977 who played TV cop Ken Hutchinson.

7

A No. 1 hit in 1977 with a French title that translates as 'Love Song'

8

This 1979 single was the second of two No. 1s in the 1970s by this artist with the word 'Eyes' in the title.

Topping the charts in January 1973, this was the only No. 1 for this 'glam rock' band that achieved a total of ten top 10 hits.

This song was the UK's bestselling single for 5 weeks in 1971, then returned to No. 1 in 2002 following the death of the performer.

TOP **40**

QUIZ **12**

From 1983, the song title shared its name with a famous tennis player.

This No. 1 was a live EP in 1980 and included the song 'Skinhead Moonstomp'.

The third of three No. 1s for this band in 1984, making them the second act in chart history to top the charts with their first three releases.

This 1985 charity record was written by Michael Jackson and Lionel Richie.

This 1988 hit had a connection for *Doctor Who* fans.

The first new No. 1 of 1989 was recorded by two stars of the TV series *Neighbours*.

Topping the charts in 1987, this Mexican folk song had originally been adapted and recorded by Ritchie Valens in 1958.

A double 'A' side in 1982 with one side being 'Computer Love'.

A 1981 No. 1 whose singer was born Mary Sandeman.

The Christmas No. 1 in 1980 that paid homage to a grandparent.

ANSWERS QUIZ **11**

xxxx 1. 'Love Grows (Where My Rosemary Goes)' by Edison Lighthouse 2. 'I'd Like to Teach the World to Sing (in Perfect Harmony)' by the New Seekers 3. 'Rivers of Babylon' by Boney M 4. 'Summer Nights' by John Travolta and Olivia Newton-John (the first was 'You're the One that I Want') 5. 'Love Me for a Reason' by the Osmonds 6. 'Silver Lady' by David Soul (the first was 'Don't Give Up on Us') 7. 'Chanson d'Amour' by Manhattan Transfer 8. 'Bright Eyes' by Art Garfunkel (the first was 'I Only Have Eyes for You') 9. 'Blockbuster' by the Sweet 10. 'My Sweet Lord' by George Harrison

QUIZ **13**

1

In 2000, this Australian duo reached No. 1 with a song that shared its title with a Top 20 hit from 1988 by the Voice of the Beehive.

2

Taken from her 2009 album *Turn It Up*, this artist got to No. 1 with this song at the age of just 18.

3

This was the first new No. 1 of 2003 and was recorded by the winner of BBC's *Fame Academy* television series.

4

In 2004, this band had the UK's bestselling single for two weeks with their double 'A' sided hit '3AM' and which other song?

5

A hit in 2002 for the actress who played Felicity Scully in the TV series *Neighbours*.

6

A Top 40 hit in 1993 but re-released in 2019 in a successful attempt to prevent the *X Factor* winner reaching No. 1.

7

This song had first reached No. 1 in 1989 for the Bangles, but then returned to No. 1 in 2001 for another chart act.

This No. 1 from September 2008 had become the second most downloaded single of all time in the UK by September 2009. It was followed by the band's Top 3 hit 'Use Somebody'.

This No. 1 was a reworked and slightly retitled version of a Top 10 hit from 1996 by Bone Thugs-n-Harmony.

Topping the charts in the year 2000, the song was featured in the movie *The Beach* staring Leonardo DiCaprio and Tilda Swinton.

QUIZ **14**

1

Written by Damien Rice, this song topped the charts in 2011 for the first girl group to win the TV show *The X Factor*.

2

Originally a Top 20 hit in 1985 for Starship, this adapted version was the Christmas No. 1 in 2018.

3

The debut release and No. 1 by a DJ whose real name is Bruce Fielder, who in 2015 took inspiration from the Jackson 5's 1970 Top 10 hit 'ABC'.

4

This 2010 No. 1 was about getting hugs from lightning bugs and was written, produced and performed by frontman Adam Young.

5

From 2018, this was the third single and first No. 1 from this Scottish singer's EP 'Breach', and it was later also included on the album *Divinely Uninspired to a Hellish Extent*.

6

This Canadian singer spent a month at No. 1 in 2012 with a song that appeared both on her EP 'Curiosity' and her album *Kiss*.

7

In 2016, this performer's record featured Wizkid and Kyle and spent 15 weeks at the top of the charts, the most time at No. 1 since Wet Wet Wet in 1994.

(((**8**)))

This Swedish DJ and producer spent three weeks at No. 1 in 2013 with a song that was both co-written and featured the voice of Aloe Blacc.

(((**9**)))

The singer wrote this with Andrew Lloyd-Webber to become the official song to celebrate the Queen's Diamond Jubilee in 2012.

(((**10**)))

In 2019, this singer became the first female to replace herself at No. 1 with her previous single '7 Rings'

QUIZ **15**

One Word No.1s, 1960-9

For the next six quizzes, all the records have one-word titles and topped the UK charts in the given decade. Can you, with the help of a few clues, name the songs and the acts that performed them?

(((1)))

The eighth UK No. 1 for this singer, topping the charts in 1961 for four weeks with an old Italian song called 'Turna a Surriento', given English lyrics by Doc Pomus and Mort Shuman.

(((2)))

The record that knocked the answer to question 1 off No. 1 in the UK was the first hit and only No. 1 for this performer born in Grand Rapids, Michigan.

(((3)))

Written by John Lennon and Paul McCartney and recorded by the Beatles on their album *Rubber Soul*, this 1966 cover version was the only hit for this group.

(((4)))

From 1961, this became the fourth and final No. 1 for one of the most successful duos of the 1960s. It was a song originally sung by Bing Crosby in the 1933 movie *Going Hollywood*.

(((5)))

It was seven years after his first hit in 1962 with 'Sheila' that this singer achieved his one and only No. 1, but that accolade lasted for only one week.

(((6)))

The lead singer of this group built his stage act around this 1968 hit with his outlandish makeup and burning headpiece.

7

The song was originally released in 1964 as the 'B' side to a track called 'Tell Me Girl' but DJs began flipping it, creating the only No. 1 for this act.

8

This version of an old spiritual became No. 1 in 1961 in both the UK and USA and was covered by Lonnie Donegan under a slightly longer title.

9

In 1967, this song gave the group of brothers their first UK No. 1, although they had written it with the Seekers in mind.

10

This 1961 No. 1 started life as a German song with English lyrics later added by Norman Newell under the name of David West. The original version was recorded by Austrian singer Lolita.

QUIZ **16** One word No.1s, 1970–9

1

Just one week at the top of the charts for this singer in 1977, with a song that won him a Grammy for 'Best Country Vocal Performance'.

2

Another record that spent just one week at No. 1 for one-hit wonders Max West and Jeffrey Calvert, who recorded this song in 1975 under what collective name?

3

Spending two weeks at No. 1 in 1972, this single was inspired by the daughter of the singer-songwriter's manager, Gordon Mills.

4

A No. 1 in 1979 for two weeks and taken from the group's album *Spirits Having Flown*.

5

This Dutch group were originally named Sweet Reaction but changed their name before recording this 1976 international hit that sold over 5 million copies worldwide.

6

Before becoming a solo artist, this singer was a member of Stevie Wonder's backing vocal group, Wonderlove. She reached No. 1 with this song in 1977.

This record spent three weeks as the UK's bestselling single in February 1975 and gave Alan Parsons his first No. 1 as a producer.

Written by Joni Michell as a tribute to one of the world's most famous music festivals after she had been talked out of attending.

First recorded by the Sutherland Brothers, this 1975 month-long No. 1 version was released as a single against the wishes of the singer.

The female lead vocals on this 1977 No. 1 were by Sandra Stevens and Nicky Stevens, who were unrelated but were members of the group at the time.

TOP **40**

QUIZ **17**   One word No.1s, 1980–9

1

The title song from a 1980 movie in which this singer played Coco Hernandez topped the charts in 1982 for three weeks. This was due to the success of the spin-off TV series, in which the singer declined the offer to reprise her role.

2

The song had been recorded in 1978 for the singer's album, *Chain Lightning*. At the time his record label refused to issue it as a single because they thought it too slow but by 1980 they had changed their minds.

3

This song spent four weeks as the UK's No. 1 in 1985 but was a relative failure in this family group's native America, where it staggered to No. 75.

4

In 1980, this single (with its nod to the Beatles 'Taxman') became the second of this trio's four No. 1s.

5

After seven years of producing hit singles and albums, in 1988 this Irish band finally reached No. 1 in the UK charts with their ninth Top 40 hit, but just for one week.

6

This remixed version of a track from the album *Actually* became the fourth UK No. 1 for this duo, spending three weeks as the UK's bestselling single in 1988.

7

The title song to a 1980 movie starring Gene Kelly that received scathing reviews from critics, some saying it was saved only by the soundtrack.

8

A 1987 No. 1 hit written and produced by Stock, Aitken and Waterman for a duo who made their chart debut the previous year with 'Showing Out (Get Fresh at the Weekend)'.

9

Released in 1984 both as a standard single in a picture sleeve and as two separate square-shaped picture discs, each with one of this successful duo's heads so many of their fans would purchase both, almost guaranteeing a No. 1.

10

A chart debut and surprise hit in 1988, spending just one week at No. 1 but winning the BRIT Award in 1989 for 'Best Single'.

QUIZ 18

One word No.1s, 1990–9

1

This was the group's 1999 comeback hit after they re-formed, making them the first act to achieve a No. 1 in the 1970s, 1980s and 1990s.

2

Topping the charts for just one week in 1996, the track features rapper Cee who co-wrote the song with the singer, Andy Whitmore and Wayne Hector (who has written over 30 hits for artists including Westlife, One Direction and Olly Murs).

3

The title song to this Jamaican artist's 1995 third album also featured in a popular TV commercial for jeans.

4

This was released in 1997 as a double 'A' side with 'Who Do You Think You Are' entering the charts at No. 1 and remaining at the top for three weeks.

5

In 1995, this record spent four weeks at the top of the charts. It was the act's first and only No. 1 and the lead single from the No. 1 album *Life*.

6

Released in 1998, this was the title track from this singer's twenty-second solo studio album and is recognised as the highest-selling single by a solo female artist in the UK.

7

Topping the charts in 1994, this track not only featured in commercials for the same product as question three, but was later used to introduce coverage of the Scottish Premier League between 1998 and 2002 by Sky Sports.

8

First released in 1994 but didn't top the charts until the following year for this Italian act that featured brothers Paolo and Gianni Visnadi, who also had hits as members of dance group Alex Party.

9

In 2005, a court ruled that the opening four bars of this 1998 No. 1 had been plagiarized from a song by a Belgium composer and ordered the withdrawal of any remaining discs in that country but that decision has since been overturned.

10

Another No. 1 that featured in a TV advert for jeans, which helped it enter the charts at No. 1 at the beginning of 1996. It was the debut hit for this chart act whose vocalist was called Jas Mann.

TOP 40

ANSWERS QUIZ **17**

1. 'Fame' by Irene Cara 2. 'Crying' by Don McLean 3. 'Frankie' by Sister Sledge 4. 'Start' by the Jam 5. 'Desire' by U2 6. 'Heart' by Pet Shop Boys 7. 'Xanadu' by the Electric Light Orchestra with Olivia Newton-John 8. 'Respectable' by Mel and Kim 9. 'Freedom' by Wham! 10. 'Perfect' by Fairground Attraction

QUIZ 19

One word No.1s, 2000–9

1

In 2007, this song became the tenth No. 1 hit for this act and their second No. 1 since reforming and beginning a second chart career in 2006. It later featured in several commercials for a leading supermarket company.

2

A debut release in 2006 by a duo from Atlanta, Georgia, that topped the charts for nine weeks, the first record to do so in over ten years.

3

In 2005, this was the first all-Welsh group to reach No. 1 since the Manic Street Preachers. This song became the band's first No. 1. The title is the name of a building in New York, although it doesn't feature in the song's lyrics.

4

The song was written and produced by Linda Perry, formerly of 4 Non Blondes, but which former Mouseketeer sang this 2003 No. 1 hit about self-esteem?

5

Released in 2004 and co-written by Cathy Dennis this song was initially offered to Kylie Minogue for her album *Body Language*. The video was banned by some TV stations because it was considered too raunchy. It won a Grammy for Best Dance record.

6

This song was originally called 'Brandy' and recorded by its co-writer, Scott English. Retitled, it became a hit for a singer and pianist in the 1970s and then a No. 1 in 2003 for this chart act.

7

This song from the year 2000 sampled Bob Dylan's 'Knocking on Heaven's Door', the first time Dylan ever sanctioned one of his songs being used this way. It gave the singer her second No. 1.

8

In 2008, this song became the band's first and only No. 1 hit to date and is the opening track of this group's second album, *Yours Truly, Angry Mob*.

9

This singer's father reached No. 1 in 1981. Twenty years later the son sold over 8 million copies of this song worldwide, making it one of the bestselling singles of all time.

10

This was the debut single for a Scottish singer who came third in the first series of *Pop Idol* in 2002. It spent two weeks at No. 1.

QUIZ 20 One word No.1s, 2010–19

1

This song was written, produced and performed by the artist and became the most successful song worldwide of 2014 with sales and equivalent streams of 14 million. The song reached No. 1 in the UK on three separate occasions during the first few months of that year.

2

In 2014, the performer of question one also co-wrote this song with the artist and produced the record as well as providing backing vocals. It shares the same one-word title as a No. 1 from 2012.

3

This 2019 song, No. 1 for a total of six weeks, became the second collaboration between a Canadian and a Cuban-born artist and came three years after their duet 'I Know What You Did Last Summer', which just missed the Top 40.

4

This singer won *The X Factor* in 2013 and topped the charts with this, her first single, a cover of a song that had previously charted for Demi Levato.

5

Swedish singer Zara Larsson featured on this 2017 No. 1 hit for a group that combines classical, electronic and dance music. Its title is closely linked to one of those styles.

6

This 2013 No. 1 was the first single taken from the singer's

No. 1 album *Prism*, and by 2020 the artist had become the first female performer to reach 3 billion views for the accompanying video.

Written by Cathy Dennis and Eg White, which female singer made her debut chart appearance with this No. 1 song in 2010, taken from her debut album *Songs from the Tainted Cherry Tree*?

The song was featured in a 2011 TV commercial for technology company Hewlett-Packard and became this act's first No. 1 single. The track features on their No. 1 debut album *Welcome Reality*.

Topping the charts in 2012, this song became the singer's first No. 1 since 'Radio' in 2004.

This 2015 single spent ten weeks at No. 1 in America and was the singer's second UK No. 1 following 2011's 'Someone Like You'.

TOP 40

QUIZ **21**

Barry, Garry or Larry

1

Can you name the singer who topped the charts in 1996 with his debut solo hit 'Forever Love'?

2

In 1982, what was the name of the act that had a No. 2 hit with the song 'Zoom'?

3

The group the Adverts had their first and only Top 20 single in 1977 with which song?

4

The hugely successful husband and wife songwriting partnership of hits such as 'I Just Can't Help Believing', 'Looking Through the Eyes of Love' and 'Saturday Night at the Movies' was Cynthia Weil and who?

5

What was the name of the harmonica player who was featured on Kate Bush's 1994 Top 40 hit, 'The Man I Love'?

6

What is the name of the Jamaican singer who achieved his biggest hit in the early months of 1977 with 'Sideshow'?

7

In 1966, the record 'Ballad of the Green Berets' made the UK Top 40, but can you name the American soldier who recorded it?

8

Under what name did Harry Hyams record his only hit, the 1975 single 'Don't Throw It All Away'?

9

According to Del Shannon's 1961 Top 10 single, who should we take our 'Hats Off to ...'?

10

With his On-U Sound System, who had a Top 10 hit in 1991 with 'Human Nature'?

QUIZ **22**

Which female singer featured on Youssou N'Dour's 1994 Top 3 hit,
'7 Seconds'?

From 1965, 'The Minute You're Gone' became the eighth No. 1 hit for
which singer?

The Housemartins achieved two Top 3 hits in 1986 with the No. 1
'Caravan of Love' and which other song?

On which album by the Beatles did the song 'Not a Second Time' first
appear?

What was the title of the only Top 20 hit achieved by ex-Go-Go singer
and guitarist, Jane Wiedlin?

Which American superstar made her UK Top 20 chart debut in 1966 with 'Second Hand Rose', as featured in the movie *Funny Girl*?

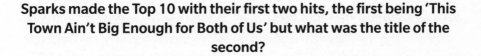

Sparks made the Top 10 with their first two hits, the first being 'This Town Ain't Big Enough for Both of Us' but what was the title of the second?

Originally a Top 30 UK hit for Smokey Robinson and the Miracles in 1968, which group had a Top 10 hit with 'I Second that Emotion' in 1982?

Which legendary songwriters were responsible for Gene Pitney's 1963 Top 10 single 'Twenty-Four Hours from Tulsa'?

According to their 1986 Top 10 song, which group claimed that they 'Can't Wait Another Minute'?

ANSWERS QUIZ **21**

1. Gary Barlow 2. Fat Larry's Band 3. 'Gary Gilmore's Eyes', 4. Barry Mann 5. Larry Adler 6. Barry Biggs 7. Staff Sergeant Barry Sadler 8. Gary Benson 9. '... Larry' 10. Gary Clail

QUIZ **23**

Red, White and Blue

Name the group that had Top 10 hits in the 1970s with 'Good Morning Freedom', 'The Banner Man' and 'Randy'.

According to the 1984 No. 1 hit, how many 'Red Balloons' belonged to Nena?

Originally a Top 3 hit for Dusty Springfield in 1964, which of her songs did the White Stripes take back into the Top 20 in 2003?

First released in 1963, who made the Top 3 in 1990 with 'Blue Velvet'?

Which song was listed alongside 'Unchained Melody' on Robson Green and Jerome Flynn's 1995 No. 1 single?

Name the group that made the Top 3 in 2002 with 'By the Way' and in 2006 with 'Dani California'.

What was the name of the act that made their Top 10 debut in 1990 with 'Naked in the Rain'?

Who wrote UB40's 1983 No. 1 hit, 'Red Red Wine'?

Two versions of the song 'A White Sport Coat (and a Pink Carnation)' made the UK Top 20 in 1957 – one was by The King Brothers but who recorded the other?

In 1997, which duo sang about 'A Red Letter Day'?

TOP **40**

QUIZ **24**

Good, Bad and Ugly

Which Liverpudlian group made the Top 20 in 1964 with 'Good Golly Miss Molly'?

'Lifestyles of the Rich And Famous' was the 2003 debut Top 10 hit for which group?

In which year was Michael Jackson's multi-million selling album *Bad* first released?

According to her 1997 Top 10 hit, who said 'A Change Would Do You Good'?

'The Ugly Duckling' was a Top 10 hit in 1975 for which actor and comedian?

The American singer Alexis Jordan had a Top 10 single in 2011 with the song 'Good ...' what?

Name the rock band that made the Top 20 in the 1970s with 'Can't Get Enough' and 'Feel Like Makin' Love'.

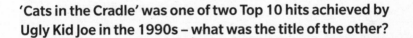

'Cats in the Cradle' was one of two Top 10 hits achieved by Ugly Kid Joe in the 1990s – what was the title of the other?

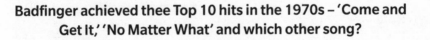

Badfinger achieved thee Top 10 hits in the 1970s – 'Come and Get It,' 'No Matter What' and which other song?

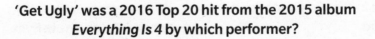

'Get Ugly' was a 2016 Top 20 hit from the 2015 album *Everything Is 4* by which performer?

ANSWERS QUIZ **23**

1. Blue Mink 2. 99 3. 'I Just Don't Know What to Do with Myself' 4. Bobby Vinton 5. 'There'll Be Bluebirds (Over) The White Cliffs of Dover' (treated as a double 'A' side with both songs listed on the sleeve, but with the label crediting side 'A' and side 'B') 6. The Red Hot Chili Peppers 7. Blue Pearl 8. Neil Diamond 9. Terry Dene 10. Pet Shop Boys

QUIZ **25**

The Danish duo Junior Senior had their first and biggest hit in 2003 with which Top 3 song?

In 1972, Argent achieved their first Top 10 hit single – what was the title?

Name the rock band that recorded 'World at Your Feet' in 2006, which became the official song for the England World Cup Squad.

In 1984, 'All Join Hands' was a Top 20 song for one of the biggest chart acts of the 1970s – name the band.

The songs '(And the) Pictures in the Sky' in 1971 and 'Slip and Slide' in 1974 were the first and last of four Top 40 hits for Medicine Head – name one of the other two, released in 1973.

Can you name the group that first made the Top 20 in 1991 with 'Fall at Your Feet'?

Which female singer and songwriter co-wrote Kylie Minogue's 2001 No. 1 hit 'Can't Get You Out of My Head'?

8

In 1990, Elton John topped the charts for five weeks with his double 'A' sided hit, 'Sacrifice' and which other song?

9

What was the title of the Top 10 single by Alanis Morissette that was taken from her album *Jagged Little Pill*?

10

From 1967, what was the title of the first Top 10 hit achieved by TV host and comedian Des O'Connor?

TOP **40**

QUIZ **26** Top, Middle and Bottom

According to their 1970 Top 10 hit, which group claimed 'I Can't Tell The Bottom from the Top'?

Although different songs, what title is shared by a 1994 Top 20 hit by Juliet Roberts and a Top 3 hit in 2002 for A1?

Name the hip-hop artist who made the American Top 10 and the UK Top 40 in 2013 with 'Started from the Bottom'.

Which successful vocal group had Top 20 hits in the 1980s with 'When She Was My Girl', 'Don't Walk Away' and 'Loco in Acapulco'?

According to their 1973 Top 10 hit, which group were 'Stuck in the Middle with You'?

First released as a 'B' side in 1968, Robert Knight had his only UK Top 10 single over the winter of 1973/4 with which song?

Which group made the UK Top 40 in 1965 with 'From the Bottom of My Heart'?

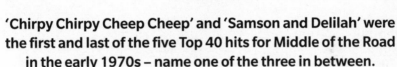

'Chirpy Chirpy Cheep Cheep' and 'Samson and Delilah' were the first and last of the five Top 40 hits for Middle of the Road in the early 1970s – name one of the three in between.

Taken from their album *Three*, which girl group made the Top 10 in 2004 with 'In the Middle'?

Name the movie that first featured the 1986 No. 1 hit by Berlin 'Take My Breath Away'.

QUIZ **27**

1

Two versions of 'This Is My Song' made the UK Top 3 in 1967 – Petula Clark's recording reached No. 1 but whose version reached No. 2?

2

Who made the Top 40 in 1989 with 'I Won't Back Down'?

3

'Lights Up' and 'Adore You' were both hits in 2019 for which singer?

4

Can you name the duo who made the UK Top 40 in 1961 with 'The Mountain's High'?

5

In 1991, which male vocalist made the UK Top 40 with his double 'A' sided hit 'It Had to Be You' and 'Recipe for Love'?

6

Can you name the trumpet player whose only UK Top 40 hit was his 1980 Top 10 hit 'Funkin' for Jamaica (NY)'?

7

Which comedian made the Top 40 in 1969 with the song 'If You Love Her'?

8

Which group, formed by Chris Frantz and Tina Weymouth of Talking Heads, had hits in the early 1980s with 'Wordy Rappinghood' and 'Under the Boardwalk'?

9

Name the singer whose hits in the 1950s included 'Island in the Sun' and the No. 1 'Mary's Boy Child'.

10

Heather Small is billed alongside which singer on the Top 40 hit 'You Need Love Like I Do' in 2000?

TOP **40**

ANSWERS QUIZ 26

1. The Hollies 2. 'Caught in the Middle' 3. Drake 4. The Four Tops 5. Stealers Wheel 6. 'Love on a Mountain Top' (his recording of 'Everlasting Love' was a Top 40 hit in both 1968 and 1974) 7. The Moody Blues 8. 'Tweedle Dee, Tweedle Dum', 'Soley Soley', 'Sacramento' 9. Sugababes 10. Top Gun

QUIZ **28**

1

'Message in a Bottle' was the first No. 1 for the Police – what was the second?

2

Name the act that had Top 10 hits in 2006 with 'I'll Be Ready' and 'First Time'.

3

From 1998, what was the title of the only major hit by French group Stardust?

4

What was the title of the studio album by the Beatles that first featured the song 'Here Comes the Sun'?

5

First released in 1985, what was the title of the only Top 10 hit achieved by the Waterboys when the record was reissued in 1991?

6

Featuring a sample of Daryl Hall & John Oates 'I Can't Go for That (No Can Do)', which chart act reached the Top 10 with 'Sunrise' in 2003?

7

What was the title of the 1978 Top 10 hit that Sarah Brightman recorded with Hot Gossip?

((8))

Italian singer Monica Bragato had her only Top 10 hit in 2002 with 'Dove (I'll Be Loving You)', which she recorded under what name?

((9))

Taken from their album *Ghost Stories*, which group made the UK and American Top 10 in 2014 with 'A Sky Full of Stars?'

((10))

From 1999, what is the title of the No. 1 hit by movie producer and director Baz Luhrmann?

QUIZ **29**

Game, Set and Match

'When You Ask About Love' was the only Top 10 hit for which successful early 1980s group?

What was the title of the song that was a No. 1 for Tommy Edwards in 1958 and Top 5 hits for both Cliff Richard in 1963 and the Four Tops in 1970?

Jaki Graham achieved two solo Top 10 hits in the mid-1980s – the first was 'Round and Round' but what was the title of the other'?

The 1977 Top 20 EP 'Spot the Pigeon' by Genesis contained three tracks: 'Inside and Out', 'Pigeons' and which other song?

Taken from their album *The Game*, which group made the Top 20 in 1980 with 'Play the Game'?

Name the group that made the Top 20 in the 1960s with 'I Put a Spell on You', 'The House that Jack Built' and 'Don't Stop the Carnival'.

Who achieved their only Top 10 hit in 1991 with 'Set Adrift on Memory Bliss'?

(((8)))

Name the Japanese trio that made the Top 20 in 1980 with 'Computer Game (Theme from The Invaders)'.

(((1)))

Kate Bush is the backing vocalist on an early 1980s Top 5 single for Peter Gabriel – what is the song and what does she sing?

(((10)))

Rob Thomas, who was the guest vocalist on Santana's hit single 'Smooth', is the vocalist and founding member of which American rock band?

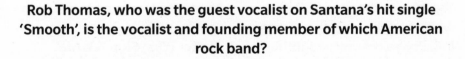

ANSWERS QUIZ **28**

1. 'Walking on the Moon', 2. Sunblock ('First Time' billed as Sunblock featuring Robin Beck as it re-mixed her 1998 No. 1) 3. 'Music Sounds Better with You', 4. *Abbey Road* 5. 'The Whole of the Moon' 6. Simply Red 7. 'I Lost My Heart to a Starship Trooper', 8. 'Moony' 9. Coldplay 10. Everybody's Free (to Wear Sunscreen) – The Sunscreen Song (Class of '99').

QUIZ **30**

1

Released in 1967 but reaching the Top 10 in February 1968, what was the title of the only hit achieved by Brenton Wood?

2

Who topped the charts in 1989 with a cover of 'Sealed with a Kiss', Brian Hyland's hit from both 1962 and 1975?

3

In 1976, Billy Ocean made the Top 20 with the song 'L.O.D.', which had the meaning of these initials as a bracketed subtitle – what did they mean?

4

Name the Swedish vocal group that had a Top 3 hit in 1994 with 'The Sign'.

5

At the very end of 2003, Blue made the Top 20 with a new version of Stevie Wonder's 'Signed, Sealed, Delivered I'm Yours' that also featured Stevie and which female singer?

6

Name the Motown act that made the Top 40 in 1969 with 'No Matter What Sign You Are'.

7

Which group had a Top 10 hit in 1983 with 'Our Lips Are Sealed'?

8

Adam and the Ants achieved two
No. 1 hits – 'Stand and Deliver' was
the first, but what was the second?

9

The last of Bryan Ferry's nine Top 40
solo hits in the 1970s came in 1978
with which song?

10

Which singer made the Top 40 in
1991 with her single 'Seal Our Fate'?

TOP **40**

ANSWERS QUIZ **29**

1. Matchbox 2. 'It's All in the Game' 3. 'Set Me Free' 4. 'Match of the Day' 5. Queen 6. The Alan Price Set 7. PM Dawn 8. Yellow Magic Orchestra 9. 'Games Without Frontiers'; she sings 'Jeux sans frontières' 10. Matchbox 20

QUIZ **31**

Remember, for the next ten quizzes, begin with 10 points, but deduct a point for each clue that you need to guess the album title and artist.

This artist's seventh studio album was released in June 1984.

The album was recorded in a period of just over two years during which time more than 80 songs were considered.

The record became the first commercial release manufactured in America on compact disc by the artist's record label; previously their CDs had been imported from abroad.

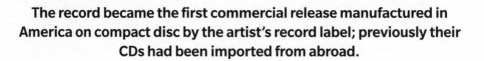

It was co-produced by Chuck Plotkin and Jon Landau in New York.

It has been alleged the artist was offered $12 million to appear in a TV commercial for the Chrysler car company and to allow the title track to be used.

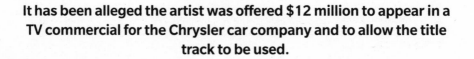

In the UK, this album spent a total of five non-consecutive weeks at No. 1.

This was the artist's most successful album and was nominated for 'Album of the Year' at the 1985 Grammy Awards ceremony.

The album cover depicted a picture of the artist's backside against the backdrop of the American flag.

In 1987, this was voted the fifth greatest rock album of all time in Paul Gambaccini's poll of over 80 critics, writers and radio broadcasters.

The album's title track was released as a double 'A' side with 'I'm on Fire', making the Top 5 in 1985.

ANSWERS QUIZ 30

QUIZ **32**

Classic Album, 2010s

1

Released on 3 March 2017 worldwide, this became the third studio album for this singer and songwriter.

2

It won a Grammy Award for 'Best Pop Vocal Album' at the sixtieth annual ceremony.

3

Entering the charts at No. 1, it was named the fastest-selling album by a male artist with sales in excess of 600,000 in downloads, streams and physical copies the first week of release.

4

Although not all were official singles, all 12 tracks made the UK Top 20 singles chart within the first week of release of the album.

5

On the day of release, the tracks on the album achieved almost 70 million streams and, by day two, videos of the songs had reached 1 billion views worldwide on YouTube.

6

Also in the week of release, the artist had all three of his albums in the chart's Top 5.

7

The song 'Perfect' became the UK's Christmas No. 1 single in 2017.

8

Two singles, 'Shape of You' and 'Castle on the Hill', were released at the beginning of 2017, debuting at No. 1 and No. 2 respectively in the same week.

9

The song 'Shape of You' has been streamed more than 1 billion times.

10

His first two albums were called + ('Plus') and × ('Multiply').

TOP **40**

ANSWERS QUIZ 31

Born in the USA by Bruce Springsteen

QUIZ **33**

This is a soundtrack album that won a Grammy for 'Album of the Year'.

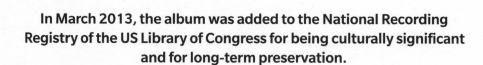

In March 2013, the album was added to the National Recording Registry of the US Library of Congress for being culturally significant and for long-term preservation.

Additional incidental music for the movie was composed and adapted by David Shire, some of which was included on the album.

This became the bestselling soundtrack album of all time, selling in excess of 40 million copies worldwide.

It topped the album charts in the UK for 18 weeks and in America for 24.

According to reliable sources, 'Lowdown' by Boz Scaggs was originally planned to be included in the movie but permission was refused for its usage.

In 2017, to commemorate the fortieth anniversary of the movie, a deluxe box version of the soundtrack was released including new mixes of some of its most successful songs (including a UK No. 1 single) along with art prints, a movie poster and a turntable mat.

(((8)))

Tavares, Yvonne Elliman and Walter Murphy & the Big Apple Band were among the artists whose music appeared in the movie.

(((9)))

The key songs in the movie were written by the Bee Gees, who also performed many of the tracks.

(((10)))

The movie starred John Travolta and catapulted him to fame.

ANSWERS QUIZ **32**

÷ ('Divide') by Ed Sheeran

QUIZ **34**

Released in October 1995, this was the band's second studio album.

It is considered a significant departure from their 1994 debut album, with more emphasis on songs with strong choruses.

The album sold almost a quarter of a million copies in the first week of release and spent a total of ten weeks at No. 1.

At the BRIT Awards in 1996, it took the prize of 'Best British Album'.

In 2010, the album was named 'The Greatest British Album since 1980' with sales in excess of 20 million worldwide.

Paul Weller provided lead guitar and backing vocals on one of the tracks, and played harmonica on another two.

During recording, tension mounted as to which of the two brothers in the band should sing lead vocals on some of the tracks.

The album cover depicted DJ Sean Rowley and sleeve designer

Brian Cannon passing each other in a London Street popular for record shops at that time. The album's producer can be seen in the background holding the master tapes in front of his face.

The band were involved in what was labelled 'The Battle of Britpop' with rival act Blur.

The first single, 'Some Might Say', was released nearly six months before the completed album.

ANSWERS QUIZ 33

Saturday Night Fever by Various Artists

TOP 40

QUIZ **35**

1

One of the songs features the sound of seagulls, which was created by a band member's laugh being played backwards.

2

Immediately following the release of this album, the act found it was unable to perform the songs live due to their complexity.

3

The longest track on the album ran for just over three minutes.

4

The group weren't officially under contract with their record label when they recorded this album as their previous deal had expired.

5

The album sleeve won a coveted Grammy Award for its designer, Klaus Voormann.

6

The album was released on 5 August 1966.

7

Three of the songs were omitted for the American release.

(((**8**)))

All tracks were produced by George Martin.

(((**9**)))

Two of the songs were released as a No. 1 double 'A' side, but that was to be the only single from the album.

(((**10**)))

The first track they recorded for the album was 'Tomorrow Never Knows'.

QUIZ **36**

Classic Album, 1970s

1

The album was released in January 1970 and was the fifth and final studio album for this act.

2

The name of title track was inspired by a song recorded by the Swan Silvertones and it's understood that Claude Jeter from the gospel group was paid compensation for the usage.

3

The title track has often been compared to 'Let It Be' by the Beatles and has been covered by over 50 different artists including Elvis Presley and Aretha Franklin.

4

It's been reported the duo had to decline an invitation to perform at the Woodstock festival due to their commitment to complete the album.

5

In 1971, the record won a Grammy for 'Album of the Year', as well as 'Best Engineered Recording', while its title track won the Grammy for 'Record of the Year', 'Song of the Year', 'Contemporary Song of the Year' and the 'Instrumental Arrangement of the Year'.

6

The story of the making of the album is told in the 2011 documentary *The Harmony Game*, which included interviews with the performers.

This release was the first time that an album's title track and the actual album topped the singles and album charts both in the UK and America simultaneously.

The only non-original song on the album (apart from an adaptation of a traditional Peruvian song) was a cover of the Everly Brothers' hit, 'Bye Bye Love'.

The duo had previously worked together under the name of Tom and Jerry before having hit records.

'El Condor Pasa (If I Could)', one of the songs on the album, was successfully covered by Julie Felix in 1970, and her version made the Top 20.

ANSWERS QUIZ **35**

Revolver by the Beatles

QUIZ **37**

It was this group's debut album and was released in November 1996.

This became the bestselling album worldwide in 1997, clocking up around 19 million sales in the first year and a total of over 23 million.

The group were formed following an advert to find five performers.

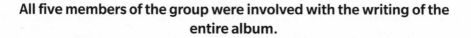

All five members of the group were involved with the writing of the entire album.

Their debut single became their only American No. 1, although they notched up a further six Top 20 hits there.

Four singles, including one double 'A' side, were released from the album, with each one topping the charts.

The main concept of the album centred on what they called 'Girl Power'.

Their collective name came about after they wrote an unreleased song called 'Sugar and Spice'.

The double 'A' side single from this album was chosen as the official 'Comic Relief' record for 1997.

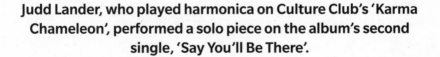

Judd Lander, who played harmonica on Culture Club's 'Karma Chameleon', performed a solo piece on the album's second single, 'Say You'll Be There'.

ANSWERS QUIZ **36**

Bridge Over Troubled Water by Simon & Garfunkel

QUIZ **38**

Classic Album, 1980s

1. Released in November 1989, this became the artist's fourth solo studio album.

The album spent a total of 15 weeks at No. 1 in the UK.

It was recognised as the bestselling album in the UK in 1990, selling just under 3 million copies.

As with some of this artist's previous albums, the sleeve notes were written in his own hand.

Eric Clapton played guitar on one of the most successful tracks to be issued as a single.

The album produced five UK Top 40 singles.

It was during this album's initial run of eight weeks at No. 1 that the 1980s turned into the 1990s.

In 2016, the album was remastered with additional studio, live and demo tracks as well as updated artwork, featuring a contemporary photo of the artist in an identical pose to the original sleeve.

9

His song 'Another Day in Paradise' won a Grammy for 'Record of the Year' and a BRIT Award for 'Best British Single'.

10

'I Wish It Would Rain Down' was the second Top 10 single from the album.

TOP **40**

ANSWERS QUIZ 37

Spice by Spice Girls

QUIZ **39**

It was released in October 2006 and within 12 months had become the second bestselling album of the twenty-first century to that point.

At the Fiftieth Grammy Awards ceremony, this record won the 'Best Pop Vocal Album of the Year' award.

All the songs on the album were written or co-written by the artist.

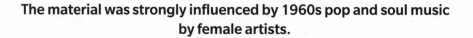

The material was strongly influenced by 1960s pop and soul music by female artists.

A total of five Top 40 singles were released from the album, two of which reached the Top 10.

This became the second and final studio album for this singer and songwriter.

One of the songs gives Nicholas Ashford and Valerie Simpson a writing credit due to the sampling of their song, 'Ain't No Mountain High Enough'.

The inspiration for the songs came during a pre-marital break from a tumultuous relationship with a partner.

The singer died on the 23 July 2011, aged just 27.

The song 'Rehab' became the biggest hit taken from the album.

ANSWERS QUIZ **38**

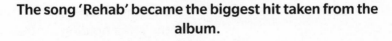

But Seriously … by Phil Collins (the single mentioned in clue 5 is 'I Wish It Would Rain Down')

QUIZ **40**

1

This became the artist's ninth studio album and his fourth to top the album charts, where it remained for four weeks.

2

One of the tracks was the first time the artist included an instrumental on one of his albums.

3

His record label wanted to call the album 'Love Is All There Is'.

4

Most of the album was recorded over a period of just four days in Nashville.

5

He introduced his fans to a new, softer singing voice, having recently given up smoking temporarily.

6

The album included a song the artist had written for the movie *Midnight Cowboy* – it was subsequently rejected but it still became a Top 10 hit.

7

The album sleeve had a picture of the artist holding a guitar and tipping his hat.

8

Johnny Cash wrote a poem to the artist that was featured on the back of the album sleeve.

9

Johnny Cash sang 'Girl from the North Country' as a duet. It was the album's opening track.

10

'Lay Lady Lay' became the biggest hit single to be taken from the album.

TOP **40**

ANSWERS QUIZ **39**

Back to Black by Amy Winehouse

Are the questions beginning to get a little taxing? Well then, try these three groups of questions for size.

To start, there's 'Superstars' (quizzes 1–10) – questions on ten multi-million-selling chart acts from over the decades.

Then there's 'Alternate Title' (quizzes 11–20) – the titles of ten hit singles provide the themes for each set of questions. (A little bit of editorial licence might have been taken with one or two questions or answers!)

Finally, 'Who Am I' (quizzes 21–30). This might seem a little easy as you work through the clues – but if you want to score highly, take your time thinking about each clue. Try and guess who the chart star is from a set of ten clues. These start cryptic, lateral or just plain obscure, but end with something 'smack-in-the-face' obvious. With each extra clue you need, you lose a point. As with the 'Classic Albums' in the previous section, if you guess correctly after just one clue, you score 10 points; after two, you score 9 points, etc. If it takes all ten clues, then you'll just score 1 point (and you might like to consider a little bit of chart revision before moving on to the Top 20!).

TOP
30

QUIZ **1**

Kylie Minogue

Which single from the year 2000 became Kylie's first No. 1 since 'Tears on My Pillow' in 1990?

... and which successful singer, dancer & choreographer co-wrote the answer to question one?

What is the name of the singer who duetted with Kylie on their 1991 Top 5 hit 'If You Were With Me Now'?

Name the Top 3 follow-up single to her debut No. 1 hit 'I Should Be So Lucky'.

What was the name of her character in the Australian soap opera *Neighbours*?

Golden is the title of her 2018 album, but what is the title of the first single released from it?

What is the name of Kylie's hit-making sister?

In which 2001 movie did Kylie appear as 'The Green Fairy'?

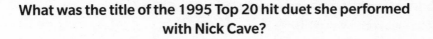

What was the title of the 1995 Top 20 hit duet she performed with Nick Cave?

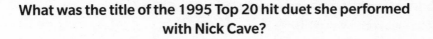

Which 1980 Kool and the Gang Top 10 hit did Kylie take back into the Top 20 in 1992?

ANSWERS QUIZ 40

Nashville Skyline by Bob Dylan (the instrumental in clue 2 is 'Nashville Skyline Rag'; the song in clue 6 is 'Lay Lady Lay')

QUIZ 2

One Direction

1

What is the title of the group's 2011 debut hit and first No. 1?

2

As of the end of 2019, two of the original five members of 1D have had solo No. 1 singles – name both of them (with extra points if you know the song titles).

3

Which Blondie song featured in their 2013 No. 1 for 'Red Nose Day' alongside 'Teenage Kicks' by the Undertones?

4

Which band member released a No. 1 album in 2020 called *Heartbreak Weather*?

5

What type of … *Memories* feature in the title of the group's 2013 No. 1 album?

6

What is the first name of Liam Payne's son?

7

Name the record label, founded by Simon Cowell, on which the group's singles and albums are released?

8

The group's most recent Top 10 single is a 2015 song that shares the same title as hits by Mai Tai in the 1980s, the Verve in the 1990s and Funeral for a Friend in the 2000s – what is that shared title?

9

Louis Tomlinson appeared on *The X Factor* in 2018 as coach to the 'Boys' – which singer in his category won the series?

10

Harry Styles played the character 'Alex' in which war film directed by Christopher Nolan?

QUIZ **3**

David Bowie

What was the name of the fictitious group that accompanied Bowie's character Ziggy Stardust?

His international No. 1 album *Let's Dance* in 1983 was accompanied by a world tour. What was the name of that tour?

Under whom did David study dance and mime in the late 1960s?

What is the title of Bowie's final studio album, released in 2016?

Name the character he played in Jim Henson's 1986 film *Labyrinth*?

His son is a successful film director, whose work includes *Moon*, *Source Code* and *Warcraft: The Beginning* – what is he called?

7

What are the titles of the three studio albums collectively known as his 'Berlin Trilogy' from the second half of the 1970s?

8

Bowie was cast in the title role of an early 1980s BBC television adaptation of which Bertolt Brecht play?

9

The lead singer of Herman's Hermits in the 1960s had a solo hit in 1971 with his song 'Oh! You Pretty Things', slightly retitled as 'Oh You Pretty Thing' – who is he?

10

Two parts: Name both No. 1s by Bowie that mention his character 'Major Tom'; and name both the German singer and his 1983 European hit which paid homage to this character?

ANSWERS QUIZ **2**

1. 'What Makes You Beautiful', 2. Zayn Malik (billed as Zayn), 'Pillowtalk'; Harry Styles, 'Sign of the Times', 3. 'One Way or Another' (official title: 'One Way or Another (Teenage Kicks)') 4. Niall Horan 5. Midnight... 6. Bear 7. Syco Music 8. 'History' (all four songs are separated by ten years: 1985, 1995, 2005, 2015) 9. Dalton Harris 10. Dunkirk

QUIZ 4

1

Who is the drummer in the band?

2

What is the title of the group's acclaimed 1983 live album that featured recordings from concerts in both Boston and Colorado in the USA and Sankt Goarshausen in Germany?

3

U2 had a Top 10 hit in 1995 called 'Miss Sarajevo', which they recorded under the name Passengers with Brian Eno and which opera singer?

4

Name any three of their five studio albums in the twentieth century that have one-word titles.

5

What is the real name of the band's guitarist 'The Edge'?

6

Bono was guest vocalist on a song that was a Top 20 hit in both 1986 and 1989 for Clannad – what is it called?

7

Adam Clayton and Larry Mullen had a Top 10 hit in 1996 with the theme tune to which film starring Tom Cruise?

Two parts: What single from their album *Rattle and Hum* shares its title with hits by Roxy Music, Bryan Adams and 911? Which short-lived girl group recorded a cover of this U2 song for a Top 20 hit in 2002?

Which legendary guitarist featured alongside the band on their Top 10 song 'When Love Comes to Town'?

Name both of the songs U2 performed at 'Live Aid' in 1985?

QUIZ **5**

What was the title of Rihanna's first UK hit single?

Which male vocalist featured on her 2008 Top 20 hit 'Rehab'?

On which Caribbean island was Rihanna born?

What is the title of her 2006 studio album, which included the hits 'SOS', 'We Ride' and 'Unfaithful'?

Name the rapper who joined her on the 2007 No. 1 hit 'Umbrella'.

What 2008 No. 1 for Rihanna has the same title as a 1994 Top 20 song by Madonna?

Featuring Rihanna, 'Love the Way You Lie' was a Top 3 hit in 2010 for which rapper?

What was the title of the 2012 movie in which she starred as Petty Officer Cora Raikes?

What is the title of the song she recorded along with Bono, the Edge and Jay-Z in 2010, in aid of the Haiti earthquake appeal?

Which American band featured Rihanna on their 2017 comeback single 'Lemon'?

QUIZ **6**

Ed Sheeran

1

As well as featuring alongside Burna Boy on Stormzy's No. 1 'Own It', Ed had three No. 1 duets of his own in 2019 – one each with Justin Bieber, Khalid and Stormzy. Name one of these three songs.

2

In which Yorkshire town was Ed born?

3

In which Australian TV series did Ed appear in 2015 as a singer-songwriter called Teddy?

4

Which song won him 'Best Song Musically and Lyrically' at the Ivor Novello Awards in 2012?

5

Name the American actor who played an important role in helping Sheeran early in his career by inviting him to play at his Los Angeles club?

6

As of the end of 2019, which of the four most commonly used mathematical symbols is yet to provide Ed with the title of a hit studio album?

7

What is the name of the record label he founded in 2015 that released Jamie Lawson's self-titled No. 1 album?

Which actor stars in the video to Ed's song 'Lego House'?

Ed Sheeran played himself in a film directed by Danny Boyle about a singer-songwriter who realizes no-one in the world apart from himself has heard of the Beatles – what is the film called?

For which Irish vocal group did Ed co-write the songs 'Dynamite', 'Better Man' and 'Hello My Love'?

TOP **30**

QUIZ **7**

1

What is the title of the 2017 Top 3 collaboration between Coldplay and the American duo the Chainsmokers?

2

Who is the bass guitarist in the group?

3

What hit single for the group shares the same title as a Top 20 single for George Benson in the 1980s and a Top 10 one for Natalie Imbruglia in the 2000s?

4

The group's 2005 Top 10 song 'Talk' includes melodic aspects of a 1981 song called 'Computer Love' by which group?

5

What is the title of the group's seventh studio album, released in 2015, that includes credits for Beyoncé, Noel Gallagher and Barack Obama?

1

In 2003, Chris Martin recorded an acoustic version of the song '2000 Miles' on the group's website with proceeds from the download going to charity. Which group recorded the original hit version in 1983?

7

What is the title of the group's original Christmas song released in 2010?

((8))

How many times have Coldplay won the award for 'Best British Group' at the BRIT Awards?

((9))

With whom did Chris Martin have a 'conscious uncoupling' in 2014?

((10))

What are the names of the two halves of the group's 2019 double album *Everyday Life*?

QUIZ **8**

Tina Turner

What is the title of the song Tina wrote that was a Top 5 hit for Ike & Tina Turner in 1973?

In 1985 Tina had a hit duet called 'It's Only Love' with which Canadian artist?

Who played Tina in the 1993 film of her life, *What's Love Got to Do with It?*

Name her 1989 No. 1 album that includes the hit singles 'The Best', 'I Don't Wanna Lose You' and 'Steamy Windows'.

What is Tina's birth name?

Who is the featured vocalist on Tina's 1996 hit version of the song 'In Your Wildest Dreams'?

Turner's final two Top 40 singles came in the 2000s – name either of these songs.

What character did Tina play in the 1975 film version of the Who's rock opera *Tommy*?

Who wrote the title track of her album *Private Dancer*, a song that was also a hit single for Tina in 1984?

Lulu was one of the co-writers of which 1993 Top 10 single for Tina?

QUIZ 9

Paul McCartney

1

Paul married his first wife in 1969 – who is she?

2

The 1977 No. 1 'Mull of Kintyre' was a double 'A' side with which other song?

3

What is the title of the 1984 Top 3 single billed as 'Paul McCartney and the Frog Chorus'?

4

What is the name of the experimental duo he created with producer and Killing Joke member Youth?

5

Which two planets feature in the title of the 1975 studio album by Wings?

6

Deemed one of the most important moments in pop music, in which year did Paul first meet John Lennon?

7

Which songwriter co-wrote four of the tracks, including the single 'My Brave Face', on the original 1989 release of his album *Flowers in the Dirt*?

TOP **30**

8

In 1979, the singer Phoebe Snow had her only UK hit with a version of a song Paul wrote and recorded on his 1970 debut solo album *McCartney* – what is the song?

9

What is the name of his brother, who was both a member of the Scaffold and had a solo hit in 1974 with the song 'Leave It'?

10

What type of '… Night' did Paul sing about on his 1997 hit single?

ANSWERS QUIZ **8**

1. 'Nutbush City Limits' 2. Bryan Adams 3. Angela Bassett 4. *Foreign Affair* 5. Anna Mae Bullock 6. Barry White (Antonio Banderas had featured on the original album version of the song) 7. 'Whatever You Need' (2000), 'Open Arms' (2004) 8. The Acid Queen 9. Mark Knopfler 10. 'I Don't Wanna Fight'

QUIZ **10**

Ariana Grande

1

In which Floridian city was Grande born?

2

Grande's first UK No. 1 came in 2014 with the song 'Problem' – it featured which Australian rapper and singer?

3

What is the title of the 2014 No. 1 she recorded with Jessie J and Nicki Minaj?

4

What was the name of Ariana's character in the Nickelodeon TV series *Victorious*?

5

Name the French DJ (and chart act in his own right) credited as one of the co-writers on her Top 3 hit 'One Last Time'?

Ariana's third studio album (released in 2016) was her first to reach No. 1 in the UK – it is called *Dangerous* ... what?

... and what is 'God ...' according to the title of her 2018 Top 5 song?

Name one of the other two singers featured alongside Ariana on the 2019 Top 3 hit 'Don't Call Me Angel (Charlie's Angels)'?

Which American music publication recognized her as 'Woman of the Year' in 2018?

What 1992 song by Céline Dion and Peabo Bryson was covered by Ariana with John Legend in 2017?

ANSWERS QUIZ 9

1. Linda McCartney (Linda Eastman) 2. 'Girls' School' 3. 'We All Stand Together' 4. The Fireman 5. *Venus and Mars* 6. 1957 7. Elvis Costello 8. 'Every Night' 9. Mike McGear 10. 'Beautiful ...'

QUIZ **11**

DJ
(Turn your radio on)

1

'Last Night a DJ Saved My Life' in 1983 was the only Top 40 hit for which American group?

2

When Robbie Williams released his single 'Radio' in 2004, did it become his sixth, eighth or tenth No. 1 since leaving Take That?

3

The late 1970s single 'On My Radio' was the first of four original hits for the 2 Tone group Selecter. The other three all came in 1980 – name one of them.

4

Which comedian reached the Top 40 in 1961 with the single 'Transistor Radio'?

5

In 2006, Corinne Bailey Rae had a Top 3 single called 'Put Your ...' what?

6

David Bowie's single 'DJ' was taken from the third of the three studio albums known as his 'Berlin Trilogy'. What is the name of that parent album?

7

The song 'Radio Radio' was a Top 40 hit in 1978 for which chart act?

8

The veteran DJ Tony Blackburn reached the Top 40 hit in 1968 with a song called 'So Much ...' what?

Known in the UK as a 'turntable hit' in its day, the 1979 single 'Pilot of the Airwaves' was a 1980 Top 20 hit in America for which British singer-songwriter?

Tom Robinson had his final Top 40 hit in 1983 with which song?

TOP **30**

QUIZ **12**

The single 'Marlene on the Wall' is the title of the first Top 40 hit for which American singer-songwriter?

The 1977 single 'Hollywood' was the fourth and final chart hit for which American singer and guitarist?

Which actor and director's name provided the title of a 2001 Top 5 single by Gorillaz?

What nationality is the singer Harpo, whose only UK hit came in 1976 with the song 'Movie Star'?

Justin Timberlake had a Top 3 hit and spent over six months in the Top 40 in 2016 with a song from the movie *Trolls*, for which he also provided the voice for the character Branch – what is the song called?

Who comes next in this sequence of chart acts – Tina Turner, Sheryl Crow, Garbage … who?

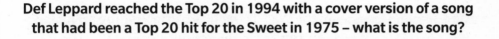

Def Leppard reached the Top 20 in 1994 with a cover version of a song that had been a Top 20 hit for the Sweet in 1975 – what is the song?

8

A Hard Day's Night is the title of the first feature film starring the Beatles – what is the title of the second?

9

Having had three Top 40 singles (including one No. 1 in 1979), the 1980 single 'Elstree' stalled at No. 55 and became the final chart entry for which chart act?

Kate Winslet had a Top 10 hit in 2001 with the theme song from the film *Christmas Carol: The Movie* in which she starred – what is the song called?

QUIZ **13**

Which group sang about 'Pineapple Head' on their 1994 single?

What was 'Frozen ...' according to the title of Peter Sarstedt's 1969 Top 10 single?

The group that began its chart career with the Top 10 song 'Love Is Life' on RAK Records in 1970 had previously been signed to the Beatles' Apple label where they recorded a version of 'Give Peace a Chance' – name the group.

What was the colour of the scarf worn by the man at the party in Carly Simon's 'You're So Vain'?

Rose McDowell and Jill Bryson had a Top 5 hit in the mid-1980s with the song 'Since Yesterday', which they recorded under what name?

The track 'Mr Sleaze' is credited alongside which 1987 Top 3 hit for Bananarama?

Which chart act thought it was 'Nice Weather for Ducks' according to the title of their 2003 hit single?

8

Who had a Top 20 song in 1993
called 'Peach'?

9

... and what 'fruit' is the colour of
the '... Beret' in the Top 40 hit for
Prince and the Revolution in 1985?

10

A northern soul hit by Rodger
Collins with the subtitle '(But I Like
It)' reached the Top 40 in 1976 –
what is its full title?

TOP **30**

ANSWERS QUIZ **12**

1. Suzanne Vega 2. Boz Scaggs 3. Clint Eastwood 4. Swedish (real
name Jan Svensson) 5. 'Can't Stop the Feeling!' 6. Madonna (singers
of the four theme songs for the Pierce Brosnan James Bond films) 7.
'Action' 8. Help! 9. The Buggles 10. 'What If'

QUIZ **14**

1

The Top 20 single 'Headlines' and the Top 10 song 'Midas Touch', both from 1986, are the only two Top 40 hits for which American group?

2

'(I Remember)' is the subtitle to a 1996 hit single by Australian singer Tina Arena – what is its full title?

3

Who spent 'One Night in Bangkok' on his hit single from the musical *Chess*?

4

What is the full title of the 2003 Top 3 Christmas single by the Darkness?

5

Nocturne is the title of a 1983 hit album for one of the most successful chart groups from the late 1970s to mid-1990s – name the group.

6

What bird features in the title of both a Top 5 single and Top 10 album in 1979 by Gerry Rafferty?

7

Songs called 'Insomnia' provided different Top 40 hits in the 1990s for two chart acts beginning with the letter 'F' – name both of them.

8

What is the title of the Top 5 single by DeBarge that was one of the first major hits for songwriter Diane Warren and featured on the soundtrack to the film *The Last Dragon*?

9

... and the Diane Warren song 'Can't Fight the Moonlight' was No. 1 for LeAnn Rimes in 2000, but for which film was it the theme song?

10

What was the first single released from Simply Red's multiplatinum 1991 album *Stars*?

QUIZ **15**

Which group had a Top 10 double 'A' side in 2005 called 'I Predict a Riot' and 'Sink that Ship'?

Where did Orchestral Manoeuvres in the Dark go 'Sailing ...' according to the title of their 1991 Top 3 single?

Name the duo that sang about a 'Ship of Fools' on their Top 10 single in 1988.

Which 1973 Top 40 single by Limmie and the Family Cookin' could be said to have a nautical connection?

Which group's hits in the 2000s included the songs 'Alcoholic', 'Silence Is Easy', 'Good Souls' and 'Four to the Floor'?

The video for which 1989 hit single by Cher was filmed aboard the USS *Missouri*?

Name the Canadian singer-songwriter who sang about 'The Wreck of the Edmund Fitzgerald' on his 1977 single.

In 2007, Katie Melua reached the Top 40 with her song 'If You Were a ...' what?

Who was going to 'Cruise into Christmas' according to the title of her 1998 Top 10 single?

The 1974 Top 10 song 'Rock the Boat' by the Hues Corporation became a Top 5 cover version in 1983 for Forrest – but what other 1970s song gave Forrest another hit cover in 1983 and his only other Top 40 single?

QUIZ **16**

Dressed for Success
(Puttin' on the Ritz)

1

What type of '... Trousers' did Madness wear in 1980?

2

Which American band spent almost six months in total in the Top 40 in 2007–8 with their Top 3 song 'Hey There Delilah'?

3

Which song by the Cardigans was a Top 3 hit in 1997 and also featured in Baz Lurhmann's film *Romeo + Juliet*?

4

The songs 'Hippy Hippy Shake' and 'You're No Good' were both Top 3 singles in the first half of the 1960s for which group?

5

What was both the colour of the 'hat' and the type of 'day' Nick Heyward sang about on his 1983 solo hit?

6

The song '6 Underground' was both a Top 20 single in 1996 and a Top 10 hit in 1997 for which group?

7

Where were the Bangles 'Walking Down ...' according to the title of the group's 1987 hit?

8

Which Dutch group's only major UK hit is the 1973 single 'Radar Love'?

9

What is the title of the Shed Seven single from 1998 with the subtitle '(Walking All Over)'?

10

Ron Dante was the lead singer on the Archies' No. 1 'Sugar Sugar' in 1969, but he was in the charts at the same time as vocalist on the song 'Tracy', a Top 5 hit for which group?

TOP **30**

ANSWERS QUIZ **15**

1. Kaiser Chiefs 2. '... on the Seven Seas' 3. Erasure 4. 'Dreamboat' 5. Starsailor 6. 'If I Could Turn Back Time' 7. Gordon Lightfoot 8. '...' Sailboat' 9. Jane McDonald 10. 'Feel the Need in Me' (originally a hit for Detroit Emeralds)

QUIZ **17**

The singles 'Tuxedo Junction' in 1976 and 'Spice of Life' in 1984 are the first and last of eight Top 40 hits for which vocal group?

What German city provided the title of a 2005 Top 10 single by Editors?

The 1990 single 'I've Been Thinking About You' was the biggest hit for a group featuring the vocals of Jimmy Helms – name the group.

Simple Minds had their only UK No. 1 in 1989 with which song?

Which Danish dance act went 'From Paris to Berlin' according to the title of their 2006 Top 3 song?

Name the UK Top 3 hit for the group Paper Lace that was also a No. 1 single in America.

Which group had all four of its Top 40 singles between 1996 and 1997 with 'No One Speaks', 'Into the Blue', 'Tranquillizer' and 'Best Regrets'?

Born Fabio Roscioli, under what name did this singer record his 1983 Top 5 hit 'Dolce Vita'?

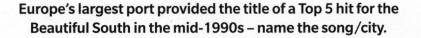

Europe's largest port provided the title of a Top 5 hit for the Beautiful South in the mid-1990s – name the song/city.

Which 1970s teeny-bop band took its name from a city in Michigan, USA?

QUIZ **18**

1

What is the title of the 1989 Top 5 hit by Kon Kan that incorporates a sample of the 1971 Top 3 hit 'Rose Garden' by Lynn Anderson?

2

The 1973 No. 1 'Tie a Yellow Ribbon Round the Old Oak Tree' is billed as being recorded by Dawn featuring … which singer?

3

The group Daisy Chainsaw had its only Top 40 hit in 1992 with which song?

4

What comes next in this sequence of studio albums by Kate Bush: *The Kick Inside, Lionheart, Never for Ever* … what?

5

The 2002 Top 40 singles '*Highly Evolved*', 'Get Free' and 'Outtathaway' and the Top 3 album *Highly Evolved* were hits for which group?

6

Name the saxophonist who featured alongside David A. Stewart on the 1990 Top 10 instrumental 'Lily Was Here'.

7

What colour '… Orchid' did White Stripes sing about on the band's 2005 Top 10 single?

8

The UK's most successful female singles artist of the 1980s carved out a secondary career in the 2000s in gardening – who is she?

What type of flower did Paul Weller sing about on his 1993 hit single?

Name the musician who played bass on Lou Reed's 'Walk on the Wild Side', David Essex's 'Rock On' and David Bowie's 'Space Oddity', and had a Top 5 single in 1980 called 'Toccata' as a member of the group Sky?

TOP **30**

QUIZ **19**

Which group had an 'Orange Crush' according to the title of their 1989 hit single?

Both of the Top 40 hits in the 1980s for Red Box reached the Top 10 – the first was called 'Lean on Me (Ah-Li-Ayo)', but what was the second?

Which band recorded the 2006 Top 3 cover of the Skids' song 'The Saints Are Coming' with U2?

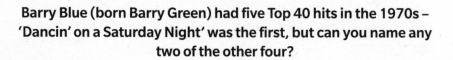

Barry Blue (born Barry Green) had five Top 40 hits in the 1970s – 'Dancin' on a Saturday Night' was the first, but can you name any two of the other four?

What '... Hill' did Coldplay sing about on the group's 2008 Top 10 song?

Having first been released in 1981, who reached the Top 20 in 1982 with 'Yellow Pearl'?

The duo Scarlet Fantastic made its only Top 40 appearance in 1987 with which song?

What was the real name of the singer Black, who recorded the Top 10 songs 'Wonderful Life' and 'Sweetest Smile'?

'(Da Ba Dee)' was the subtitle of a 1999 No. 1 for the Italian group Eiffel 65 – what was it actually called?

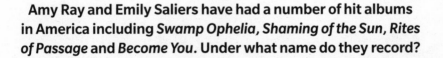

Amy Ray and Emily Saliers have had a number of hit albums in America including *Swamp Ophelia*, *Shaming of the Sun*, *Rites of Passage* and *Become You*. Under what name do they record?

QUIZ **20**

1

'Motorcycle Emptiness' was a Top 20 hit in 1992 for which Welsh group?

2

The Jags made their only Top 40 appearance in 1979 with which Top 20 song?

3

The 1989 single 'Drive On' was the fifth and final Top 40 single for which late 1980s boyband?

4

The actor David Hasselhoff reached the Top 3 in 2006 with a song that had been an Australian No. 1 for six weeks in 1976 for the Ted Mulry Gang – what is the song?

5

'Tijuana Taxi' was a Top 40 single in 1966 for which American chart act?

6

Prince's 'Little Red Corvette' was a Top 3 double 'A' side in 1985 with which other song?

7

The first hit single for Rose Royce reached the Top 10 early in 1977 – what is it called?

8

The song 'Drive By' was a worldwide hit in 2012 for which American band?

What is the title of the 1980 hit album by the Jacksons that includes the singles 'Can You Feel It?', 'Lovely One' and 'Walk Right Now'?

Which group were 'Driving with the Brakes On' according to the title of their 1995 Top 20 song?

QUIZ **21**

Who Am I?

The less clues you need to guess the artist, the more points you'll get – no peeking ahead!

1

(For 10 points) *Skyways*

2

(For 9 points) H. G. Wells

3

(For 8 points) Kristina Rihanoff

4

(For 7 points) Framing Benjamin

5

(For 6 points) PWL

6

(For 5 points) *Ten Good Reasons*

(((7)))

(For 4 points) Caractacus Potts

(((8)))

(For 3 points) 'Nothing Can Divide Us'

(((9)))

(For 2 points) Scott Robinson

(((10)))

(For 1 point) Kylie Minogue

QUIZ **22**

(For 10 points) Washington

(For 9 points) Otis, Isaac, Tara, Merlin

(For 8 points) Ceramics and art teacher in west London

(For 7 points) *Breakfast on Pluto*

(For 6 points) 'Don't You (Forget About Me)'

(For 5 points) 'Is Your Love Strong Enough?'

(For 4 points) Jerry Hall

(For 3 points) *Boys and Girls*

(For 2 points) 'A Hard Rain's Gonna Fall'

(For 1 point) Roxy Music

ANSWERS QUIZ **21**

Jason Donovan: 10 points: Made his first TV appearance aged 11 in this Australian programme **9 points:** Jason played the character Parson Nathaniel in the touring version of *Jeff Wayne's Musical Version of The War of the Worlds – The New Generation*, inspired by H. G. Wells's novel **8 points:** His partner on the 2011 series of *Strictly Come Dancing* – he finished third **7 points:** The name of the lead character's younger brother in Joseph and the Amazing Technicolor *Dreamcoat* – Jason took the lead role in 1991 West End revival of the musical **6 points:** The record label of his major hits between 1988 and 1991 **5 points:** His 1989 debut No. 1 album which sold over 1.5 million in the UK **4 points:** Donovan's character in the musical version of *Chitty Chitty Bang Bang* (2004–5) **3 points:** His first hit solo single – No. 5 in 1988 **2 points:** The name of his character in *Neighbours* **1 point:** His love interest on *Neighbours* and singing partner on the No. 1 duet 'Especially for You'

QUIZ **23**

Who Am I?

(For 10 points) Alison

(For 9 points) 'Sweet Baby James'

(For 8 points) Big Machine

(For 7 points) Reading, Pennsylvania

(For 6 points) Tim McGraw

(For 5 points) 'Fearless'

(For 4 points) Wonderstruck

(For 3 points) Bombalurina

(For 2 points) 1989

(10)

(For 1 point) 'Look What You Made Me Do'

TOP **30**

QUIZ **24**

Who Am I?

(For 10 points) Brentford

(For 9 points) Denis Law & Jimi Hendrix

(For 8 points) 'Phyllis'

(For 7 points) Market Deeping Model Railway Club

(For 6 points) *Blood Red Roses*

(For 5 points) HMS *Ark Royal*

(For 4 points) *The Great American Songbook*

(For 3 points) Penny Lancaster

(For 2 points) The Faces

(For 1 point) 'Da "Ya" Think I'm Sexy?'

ANSWERS QUIZ 23

Taylor Swift:
10 points: Her middle name
9 points: Taylor is named after singer-songwriter James Taylor
8 points: The record label that released her debut self-titled album
7 points: Her birthplace
6 points: Country music star whose name is the title of Taylor's first published song and debut single
5 points: The title of her debut tour which ran in 2009–10
4 points: The first fragrance (created by Elizabeth Arden) endorsed by Taylor
3 points: Her character in the 2019 film version of *Cats*
2 points: The year of her birth and also the title of her 2014 album
1 point: Title of her first UK No. 1

QUIZ **25**

(For 10 points) Cliff Richard

(For 9 points) 16 May 1966

(For 8 points) *Nutty Professor II: The Klumps*

(For 7 points) Eissa Al Mana

(For 6 points) *True You: A Journey to Finding and Loving Yourself*

(For 5 points) 1814

(For 4 points) Jimmy Jam and Terry Lewis

(For 3 points) Super Bowl wardrobe 'malfunction'

(For 2 points) *Design of a Decade: 1986–1996*

(For 1 point) 'When I Think of You'

TOP 30

ANSWERS QUIZ 24

Rod Stewart:

10 points: Rod had trials with the football club as a teenager

9 points: Rod recorded Hendrix's 'Angel' as a duet with Denis Law for the 1974 Scotland World Cup Squad album *Scotland Scotland*

8 points: Nickname given to him by Long John Baldry and used by Elton John (who is 'Sharon')

7 points: Rod, a model railway enthusiast, donated £10,000 to the club after their display was destroyed by vandals in 2019

6 points: Title of his 2018 No. 1 album

5 points: The subject of the BBC TV documentary *Sailor*, which used Rod's version of 'Sailing' as its theme song

4 points: His series of hit albums featuring American standards

3 points: His wife

2 points: The band with which he had success in the 1970s

1 point: His 1978 No. 1 single

QUIZ **26**

Who Am I?

(For 10 points) Coal Bowl Starter

(For 9 points) Carey Hart

(For 8 points) Choice

(For 7 points) Mya, Lil' Kim, Christina Aguilera

(For 6 points) You+Me

(For 5 points) Covered by Shirley Bassey in 2007 for the Welsh singer's most recent chart appearance in the UK

(For 4 points) 'True Love' – Lily Rose Cooper

(For 3 points) !

(For 2 points) *Missundaztood*

(For 1 point) 'Just Like a Pill'

Janet Jackson:

1 point: Her first US No. 1 single – she hasn't had a UK No. 1 worldwide

2 points: The title of her multi-platinum greatest hits album that has sold over 10 million copies worldwide

3 points: Infamous incident during performance at the half-time show at the Super Bowl in 2004

4 points: Writers and producers of many of her biggest hits

5 points: The number in the title of her 1989 album *Janet Jackson's Rhythm Nation 1814*

6 points: Title of her 2011 'self-help' book she co-authored with David Ritz

7 points: The name of her son born in 2017

8 points: A starring role as Denise Gaines in the film opposite Eddie Murphy

9 points: Her birth date

10 points: Janet & Cliff duetted on a 1984 single called 'Two to the Power of Love'

QUIZ **27**

Who Am I?

(For 10 points) Saginaw, Michigan

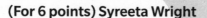

(For 9 points) Judkins

(For 8 points) Louis Armstrong, Glenn Miller, Ella Fitzgerald, Count Basie

(For 7 points) 'Alfie' by Eivets Rednow

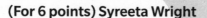

(For 6 points) Syreeta Wright

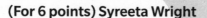

(For 5 points) Spike Lee's *Jungle Fever*

(For 4 points) **Chaka Khan, Eurythmics, Gap Band**

(For 3 points) **Paul McCartney**

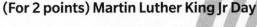

(For 2 points) **Martin Luther King Jr Day**

(For 1 point) **'You Are the Sunshine of My Life'**

TOP 30

QUIZ **28**

1

(For 10 points) *Sesame Street*

2

(For 9 points) Allah & the Knife Wielding Punks

3

(For 8 points) 'I'm Doin' Fine'

4

(For 7 points) Debbie Harry

5

(For 6 points) *Ant & Dec's Saturday Night Takeaway*

6

(For 5 points) *Adventures in the Land of the Good Groove*

7

(For 4 points) Atlantic Records

7

(For 3 points) *An Upside Down Story of Family, Disco and Destiny*

8

(For 2 points) 'Get Lucky'

10

(For 1 point) Chic

QUIZ **29**

(For 10 points) The Pleasure Seekers

(For 9 points) Leather and the Suedes

(For 8 points) Dreamland

(For 7 points) A Squeeze single from the early 1980s

(For 6 points) Detroit, Michigan

(For 5 points) 'Rolling Stone'

(For 4 points) Chris Norman

(For 3 points) Mickie Most

(((9)))

(For 2 points) Len Tuckey

(((10)))

(For 1 point) 'Can the Can'

ANSWERS QUIZ **28**

1 point: Co-founder, songwriter and producer

2 points: Co-writer and guitarist on Daft Punk's No. 1 hit

3 points: The subtitle of his autobiography Le Freak

4 points: Chic signed to Atlantic in 1977, having previously been turned down by the label

5 points: The title of his 1983 debut solo album, released just weeks before Let's Dance, David Bowie's album he co-produced

6 points: The theme tune uses the line 'I just can't wait for Saturday', which comes from the Norma Jean Wright song 'Saturday', co-written by Nile

7 points: Along with Chic partner Bernard Edwards, produced her debut solo album Koo Koo in 1981

8 points: 1973 hit for the group New York City – Nile was in their touring band

9 points: Briefly the name of Nile Rodgers and Bernard Edwards's band before forming Chic

Nile Rodgers: 10 points: Early professional gig was as a member of the touring band for the Sesame Street stage show

QUIZ **30**

Who Am I?

(For 10 points) Bishop's Stortford Junior Operatics

(For 9 points) 'Latch'

(For 8 points) 'Sound of 2014'

(For 7 points) 'Nirvana'

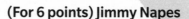

(For 6 points) Jimmy Napes

(For 5 points) Official 'Red Nose Day' single 2015

(For 4 points) *In the Lonely Hour*

(For 3 points) Naughty Boy

(For 2 points) *Spectre*

(For 1 point) 'Money on My Mind'

TOP **30**

ANSWERS QUIZ **29**

Suzi Quatro:

10 points: The name of the band she formed with her sisters in the 1960s

9 points: The name of the band her character Leather Tuscadero formed in the TV series *Happy Days*

8 points: The label she joined in 1980, set up by writers Nicky Chinn & Mike Chapman who composed most of her hits

7 points: 'Annie Get Your Gun', a 1982 single by Squeeze has the same name as the title of the West End show she starred as Annie Oakley in 1986

6 points: Her birthplace

5 points: The title of her debut solo single on RAK, a No. 1 in Portugal!

4 points: Recorded a duet with her in 1978 called 'Stumblin' In'

3 points: The producer of all her major hits

2 points: Guitarist on her hit singles in the 1970s and her first husband

1 point: Her debut hit and first No. 1

Two groups of questions to tease the brain. 'Labelled with (Indie) Love' (quizzes 1–10) is ten sets of questions about artists who have either a direct or indirect connection with a particular record label that began life as an independent. Award yourself an extra point if you can name the label. Be prepared for some brain fryers along the way!

No cheating online for the 'WWW' questions (quizzes 11–20). These are all 'Who', 'What' and 'When' questions. They range from finding the connection to guessing the year; and from working out what comes next to trying to spot who or what is missing. Some lateral or curveball thinking may be required.

TOP
20

QUIZ **1**

Labelled with (Indie) Love

Seal's 'Kiss from a Rose' features on the soundtrack to which film in the *Batman* series?

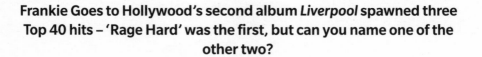

What is the name of the synth-pop group that has included Anne Dudley, Trevor Horn and Gary Langan among its members and had a Top 10 single in the mid-1980s called 'Close (to the Edit)'?

Frankie Goes to Hollywood's second album *Liverpool* spawned three Top 40 hits – 'Rage Hard' was the first, but can you name one of the other two?

'Sun Goes Down' is the title of a Top 5 song in 2008 for David ... who?

What is the title of the 1990 Top 10 single credited to MC Tunes vs 808 State?

The 1984 debut hit for the German group Propaganda takes its title from a fictional character in a 1920s German novel by Norbert Jacques and a series of films by director Fritz Lang – what is it called?

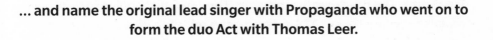

7

… and name the original lead singer with Propaganda who went on to form the duo Act with Thomas Leer.

8

One of the most successful chart singles in the 1990s for Tom Jones was a Top 20 hit in 1994 called 'If I …' what?

9

The lead singer with the Pogues had a solo hit in 1996 with his version of the classic song 'My Way' – who is he?

10

Grace Jones's concept album *Slave to the Rhythm* in 1985 featured voiceovers by which British actor?

ANSWERS QUIZ 30

Sam Smith: 10 points: Sam was a member of the company as a child. **9 points:** Sam's breakthrough as guest vocalist on the 2012 hit single by Disclosure. **8 points:** Winner of the annual BBC poll by music and industry critics. **7 points:** Not the band, but the title of Smith's EP in 2013. **6 points:** Sam's regular songwriting collaborator and producer. **5 points:** Sam recorded a No. 1 version of his song 'Lay Me Down' with John Legend for the Comic Relief charity. **4 points:** Sam's first album, which received a Guinness World Record for the most consecutive weeks in the UK Top 10 by a debut album. **3 points:** Sam provided vocals on Naughty Boy's 2013 No. 1 'La La La'. **2 points:** Sam sang the theme song 'Writing's on the Wall' for the 2015 James Bond film. **1 point:** Sam's first solo No. 1 single

QUIZ **2**   Labelled with (Indie) Love

Ian Dury & The Blockheads first reached the Top 40 in 1978 with which Top 10 single?

Prior to his 1980 solo hits 'Stop the Cavalry' and 'You'll Always Find Me in the Kitchen at Parties' on this label, Jona Lewie reached the charts as writer/vocalist of 1972 Top 3 hit 'Sea Side Shuffle' credited to which novelty group?

The American singer Rachel Sweet was just 16 when she had her only solo Top 40 hit in the late 1970s with which song?

The 1986 hit 'Brilliant Mind' was the only Top 40 appearance for which west London group?

What is the title of the lead track on the 1980 Top 10 EP 'Work Rest & Play' by Madness?

The American band Devo just missed out on a Top 40 hit in 1978, peaking at No. 41 with their version of which Rolling Stones song?

7

Prior to her chart appearances, Tracey Ullman had TV success in a comedy sketch show alongside Lenny Henry and David Copperfield – what is the title of that TV show?

8

Although he had most of his hits in the 1970s, Alvin Stardust had a Top 5 hit in 1981 with a song that had been a Top 3 hit for Nat 'King' Cole way back in 1953 – what is the song?

9

Lene Lovich had all three of her Top 40 singles in 1979 – 'Lucky Number' was the first, but can you name one of the other two?

10

The Belle Stars had a run of hits in the early 1980s, but several members of the band had originally reached the charts as members of which 2 Tone label group?

TOP **20**

ANSWERS QUIZ **1**

1. *Batman Forever* 2. Art of Noise 3. 'Warriors (of the Wasteland)', 'Watching the Wildlife' 4. David Jordan 5. 'The Only Rhyme that Bites' 6. 'Dr Mabuse' 7. Claudia Brücken 8. '... Only Knew' 9. Shane MacGowan 10. Ian McShane. LABEL: ZTT

QUIZ **3**   Labelled with (Indie) Love

The song 'Things Can Only Get Better' spent a month at No. 1 in 1994 for which chart act?

2

Peter Shelley, the writer and producer of the early hits for Alvin Stardust, had his own solo chart success with two Top 5 hits in the mid-1970s – name either of these songs.

3

Bad Manners had nine Top 40 singles on this label in the early 1980s, four of which reached the Top 10 – name any two of the Top 10 hits.

4

The 1995 Top 10 song 'Your Loving Arms' was the biggest solo hit for a German-born singer who had previously provided vocals on chart singles by S-Express and Electribe 101 – who is she?

Two different songs called 'Let's Dance' were Top 40 hits in the 1980s – one was recorded by David Bowie, but who recorded the other?

6

The 1976 single 'Get Up and Boogie' was a Top 10 hit for Silver Convention, but the group had three other Top 40 singles in the 1970s – name one of these other three.

7

In 1995, Jimmy Somerville had a hit with 'Hurt So Good', a song that had originally reached the charts 20 years earlier for which Jamaican singer?

8

The group Brendon made its one and only chart appearance in 1977 with which single released on this label?

9

Which group considered themselves the 'Midnite Dynamos' according to the title of their 1980 hit?

10

The singer Adrian Baker made his only chart appearance under his own name with a 1975 Top 10 cover of an old Four Seasons hit – name both the song and the group that was billed alongside Adrian on the label?

ANSWERS QUIZ 2

1. 'What a Waste' (the original sleeve just credits Ian Dury on the front, but the Blockheads are credited on the label) 2. Terry Dactyl & The Dinosaurs (written under his real name – John Lewis) 3. 'B-A-B-Y', 4. Furniture 5. 'Night Boat to Cairo' 6. '(I Can't Get No) Satisfaction' (which Devo slightly retitled as '(I Can't Get Me No) Satisfaction') 7. Three of a Kind 8. 'Pretend' 9. 'Say When', 'Bird Song', 10. The Bodysnatchers LABEL : Stiff

QUIZ **4**

Labelled with (Indie) Love

1

Name the lead singer with Depeche Mode who had solo hits in 2003 called 'Dirty Sticky Floors', 'I Need You' and 'Bottle Living'?

2

Which song written by Andy Bell and Vince Clarke was a Top 10 cover for the duo Dollar early in 1988, nearly two years after Erasure's original version on this label failed to reach the Top 40?

3

By what name was the duo Yazoo known in America?

4

Name the singer-songwriter who has been both a member of

Longpigs and Pulp, and released Top 10 albums in the 2010s called *Standing at the Sky's Edge*, *Hollow Meadows* and *Further*?

5

What is the title of the 2005 Top 5 single by Goldfrapp that shares the same title as the fourth and final studio album by the Faces, which reached No. 1 in 1973?

6

Who was the vocalist on 'Never Never', the 1983 Top 5 hit and only single by the Assembly?

7

What is the title of the No. 1 album by Moby that includes the hit singles 'Honey', 'Why Does My Heart Feel So Bad?', 'Porcelain' and 'Natural Blues'?

Graham Lambert and Tom Hingley are among the members of the group that had Top 20 hits in 1994 with the songs 'Saturn 5' and 'I Want You' – what is the group called?

Name both of the hit songs by Depeche Mode to have the word 'Silence' in their titles.

The group Grinderman was formed as a side project of which Australian band?

ANSWERS QUIZ 3

1. D:Ream 2. 'Gee Baby' (No. 4 in 1974), 'Love Me Love My Dog' (No. 3 in 1975) 3. 'Special Brew' (1980), 'Can Can', 'Walkin' in the Sunshine' (both 1981), 'My Girl Lollipop (My Boy Lollipop)' (1982) 4. Billie Ray Martin 5. Chris Rea (who began his chart career on this label) 6. 'Save Me', 'Fly Robin Fly' (both 1975), 'Everybody's Talkin' 'Bout Love' (1977) 7. Susan Cadogan 8. 'Gimme Some' (which had been released by the group on a different label the previous year) 9. Matchbox 10. 'Sherry', the Tonics LABEL: Magnet

QUIZ **5**   Labelled with (Indie) Love

Which group had hits in the mid-1970s with the songs 'Only You Can', 'Imagine Me, Imagine You' and 'S-S-S-Single Bed'?

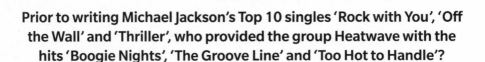

… and the lead singer of that group had her own solo Top 40 hit in 1977. Name both the singer and the song.

What is the title of the song, written by American folk and blues singer Tom Rush, that was a Top 10 hit for both the Walker Brothers in 1976 and Midge Ure in 1982?

(((4)))

Prior to writing Michael Jackson's Top 10 singles 'Rock with You', 'Off the Wall' and 'Thriller', who provided the group Heatwave with the hits 'Boogie Nights', 'The Groove Line' and 'Too Hot to Handle'?

(((5)))

The Anglo-French group Voyage is best known for its 1978 Top 20 double 'A' side 'From East to West' and 'Scots Machine', but the band did have one further Top 40 single in 1979 – what is that hit called?

Who Am I? I was born Leslie Sebastian Charles in Trinidad and Tobago in 1950, I made my UK chart debut in 1976 with 'Love Really Hurts Without You' and in 1989 while 'Licence to Kill' was in the UK charts, I was enjoying a hit in America with a song called 'Licence to Chill'?

((7))

Name the family group whose run of seven Top 40 singles began in 1977 with 'Think I'm Gonna Fall in Love with You' and ended in 1980 with 'Love Patrol'?

((8))

The song that was originally a hit for Tony Etoria in 1977 and then a Top 10 cover by Phil Fearon in 1986 is called 'I Can ...' what?

((9))

Who reached the Top 40 in 1976 with a disco version of the Barry Manilow song 'Could It Be Magic'?

((10))

The group New Musik had all three of its Top 40 singles in 1980 – 'Living by Numbers' was the first, but name one of the other two.

ANSWERS QUIZ **4**

1. Dave Gahan 2. 'Oh l'Amour' (spelt 'O l'Amour' for Dollar's release) 3. Yaz (there was already an American band called Yazoo) 4. Richard Hawley 5. 'Ooh La La'/Ooh-La-La 6. Feargal Sharkey 7. Play 8. Inspiral Carpets (the band's own imprint, Cow, was distributed through this label) 9. 'Leave in Silence' (1982), 'Enjoy the Silence' (1990; remixed in 2004) 10. Nick Cave & the Bad Seeds LABEL: Mute

QUIZ **6**

Labelled with (Indie) Love

Pete Wylie's band Wah! made its chart debut in the 1980s with the Top 3 song 'The Story of the Blues', but under what exact name did the band have its third and final hit in 1984 with 'Come Back'?

'Are "Friends" Electric?' was a 1979 No. 1 single by Tubeway Army, but what is the title of the No. 1 album from which it was taken?

... and what is the title of the only No. 1 single by Gary Numan as a solo artist?

The 1997 Top 10 singles 'North Country Boy' and 'How High', and a Top 20 single and No. 1 album both called 'Tellin' Stories', were recorded by which group?

Name both of the Top 10 singles in the 1980s for the group Freeez.

Ian McNabb is both the lead singer and songwriter on 'Love Is a Wonderful Colour', the only Top 40 hit for which group?

Which song by the Cult was originally a Top 20 hit in 1985 and then again as a remix in 1993, reaching the same chart position of No. 15 on both occasions?

The group Bauhaus had its biggest hit in 1982 with a cover of David Bowie's song 'Ziggy Stardust' – what is the name of the group's lead singer?

Prior to joining Paul Weller in the Style Council, Mick Talbot was a member of the Merton Parkas, who had their one and only Top 40 hit in 1979 with which song?

What is the name of the group that had an instrumental hit in 1982 with 'Cacharpaya (Andes Pumpsá Dèsi)'?

TOP **20**

QUIZ 7

Labelled with (Indie) Love

1

Name the band that made its chart debut in 2002 with 'What a Waster' and had further hits in 2003–4 with 'Time for Heroes', 'Don't Look Back into the Sun' and the Top 3 song 'Can't Stand Me Now'.

2

Which song written by Morrissey and Johnny Marr became Sandie Shaw's first Top 40 single in 15 years when it was released in 1984?

3

… and the Smiths only had two Top 10 singles before they disbanded in 1987 – name either of these.

4

Name the punk band from Northern Ireland whose debut album *Inflammable Material* was a Top 20 hit in 1979 and contained their signature song 'Alternative Ulster'?

5

Reading, Writing and Arithmetic is the title of the 1990 Top 5 debut album by which group?

6

The 2005 album *Funeral* by Arcade Fire included four Top 40 hits – name any two of these.

7

What is the connection between the singer of the 1973 hit single 'Free Electric Band' and the guitarist in the band that recorded the 2005 Top 5 song 'Juicebox'?

Who is the lead singer and songwriter with Scritti Politti, whose debut album *Songs to Remember* was released on this label in 1982?

The Fall reached the Top 40 in 1987 with a version of a song that had been a hit for R. Dean Taylor in 1974 – what is the song?

Robert Wyatt, who had a hit on this label in 1983 with 'Shipbuilding', had been a founding member of a band that were central to the 'Canterbury Scene' in the late 1960s and early 1970s – name the band.

ANSWERS QUIZ 6

LABEL: Beggars Banquet

1. The Mighty Wah! 2. *Replicas* 3. 'Cars' 4. The Charlatans 5. 'Southern Freeez' (1981), 'IOU' (1983) 6. The Icicle Works 7. 'She Sells Sanctuary' 8. Peter Murphy 9. 'You Need Wheels' 10. Incantation

QUIZ **8**   Labelled with (Indie) Love

Name the one-time keyboard player with Squeeze who presented both *The Tube* on Channel 4 and is host of the music show *Later* on BBC Two?

The singer-songwriter Karel Fialka is best known for which 1987 Top 10 single?

Which group had Top 40 hits in 1991 with 'The One I Love' and 'It's the End of the World as We Know It' – both originally released in 1987?

'Our Lips Are Sealed' was a Top 10 single and final hit in the UK for Fun Boy Three in 1983, but which group made its American chart debut with the song in 1981?

Who was the drummer with the Police?

Complete the title of this 1984 hit single for the Welsh band the Alarm – 'Where Were You Hiding When ...' what?

The husband and wife team of Pat and Barbara K. MacDonald founded the 1980s act that had its only hit with 'The Future's So Bright I Gotta Wear Shades' – name the act.

Prior to having a solo Top 5 single in 1986 with the song 'Camouflage', Stan Ridgway was a member of which of these bands – Wall of Voodoo, the Hoodoo Gurus or Hootie & the Blowfish?

9

Doctor and the Medics reached No. 1 in 1986 with a version of 'Spirit in the Sky' – name another Top 40 hit they had that year.

10

By what name was the group the Beat known in America?

ANSWERS QUIZ 7

1. The Libertines 2. 'Hand in Glove', 3. 'Heaven Knows I'm Miserable Now' (1984), 'Sheila Take a Bow' (1987) (a post-split 1992 reissue of the debut hit 'This Charming Man' also reached the Top 10) 4. Stiff Little Fingers 5. The Sundays 6. 'Laika' (officially 'Neighbourhood #2 (Laika)'), 'Power Out' (officially 'Neighbourhood #3 (Power Out)'), 'Rebellion (Lies)', 'Wake Up', 7. Father and son (Albert Hammond recorded 'Free Electric Band', his son Albert Hammond Jr is one of the guitarists with the Strokes, who had the hit 'Juicebox'), 8. Green Gartside 9. 'There's a Ghost in My House' (the Fall signed briefly to this label at the start of the 1980s) 10. Soft Machine LABEL: Rough Trade

QUIZ 9

Labelled with (Indie) Love

Which band recorded the seminal 1968 No. 1 album *Ogden's Nut Gone Flake*?

Who did the McCoys tell to 'Hang On ...' according to the title of the group's Top 5 hit in 1965?

'Handbags and Gladrags', which the Stereophonics covered for a Top 5 hit in 2001, had previously reached the Top 40 over the winter of 1967–8 for which singer?

Which member of Fleetwood Mac wrote the group's 1969 Top 3 single 'Man of the World'?

Who replaced Paul Jones as the lead singer with Manfred Mann in the mid-1960s?

P. P. Arnold made her first Top 40 appearance since 'Angel of the Morning' in 1968 as guest vocalist on a 1988 Top 20 hit by the Beatmasters – what is its title?

Which member of the trio Emerson, Lake & Palmer had previously been a member of the Nice?

Which band is billed alongside John Mayall on the hit albums

A Hard Road, Crusade and *Diary of a Band Volume 1*?

Following his success in Amen Corner, Andy Fairweather-Lowe went on to have two hit solo singles in the mid-1970s which reached the Top 10 – 'Wide Eyed and Legless' was one, but what was the other?

... and Amen Corner's final single on this label was a 1969 cover, which failed to chart, of a song that had been a No. 1 for the Beatles earlier in the year – what is the song?

TOP 20

QUIZ **10** Labelled with (Indie) Love

(1)

Prior to her success as a radio and TV presenter, Lauren Laverne had hits as lead singer and guitarist with a group that took its name from a character in *Grease* – what were they called?

(2)

To date, what is the title of the only UK No. 1 by Razorlight?

(3)

What is the surname of brothers Danny and Richard of the band Embrace, whose hits include the Top 10 songs 'All You Good Good People', 'Come Back to What You Know' and 'Gravity'?

(4)

What is the title of the debut No. 1 album by Keane that includes the hits 'This Is the Last Time', 'Everybody's Changing', 'Somewhere Only We Know' and 'Bedshaped'?

(5)

Which band had Top 10 songs in 1996 called 'Slight Return', 'Cut Some Rug' and 'Marblehead Johnson'?

Coldplay's first three Top 40 singles were all in 2000 and all had one word titles – 'Shiver' was the first, but what were the one-word titles of the other two?

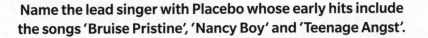

Name the lead singer with Placebo whose early hits include the songs 'Bruise Pristine', 'Nancy Boy' and 'Teenage Angst'.

Which band recorded the 1995 No. 1 album *I Should Coco*?

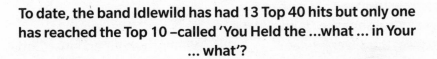

To date, the band Idlewild has had 13 Top 40 hits but only one has reached the Top 10 –called 'You Held the ...what ... in Your ... what'?

Which song, originally a Top 10 hit for Ash in 2001, became a Top 40 cover for Annie Lennox in 2009?

ANSWERS QUIZ **9**

1. The Small Faces 2. '...Sloopy' 3. Chris Farlowe 4. Peter Green 5. Mike d'Abo 6. 'Burn It Up' 7. Keith Emerson 8. Bluesbreakers 9. 'Reggae Tune' 10. 'Get Back' LABEL: Immediate

QUIZ **11**

We've decided to treat you to some extra trivia in following sets of answers, so you'll now find quizzes on every other couple of pages.

1

What's the connection – Kiki Dee, George Michael, Blue, 2Pac?

2

When was this – Elvis Presley died; Fleetwood Mac released *Rumours*; the Sex Pistols narrowly missed out on No. 1 with 'God Save the Queen' at the time of the Silver Jubilee?

3

Who comes next – Mary Wells, Kim Weston, Tammi Terrell ...?

4

What's the total – the combined total of the official line-ups of Take That on the eight studio albums released to 2019 (*Take That & Party, Everything Changes, Nobody Else, Beautiful World, The Circus, Progress, III, Wonderland*)?

5

Who's missing – Taylor, Taylor, ?, Rhodes, Le Bon?

6

What's the connection – Gloria Estefan, Jamie Cullum, Robert Knight, Worlds Apart?

7

Who or what comes next – Coldstream Guards, Status Quo, the Style Council ...?

When was this – 'Concert for George' took place at the Royal Albert Hall to mark the first anniversary of George Harrison's death; Queen's musical We Will Rock You premiered in London; Will Young's debut 'Anything Is Possible/Evergreen' sold over 1.1 million in its first week?

What's the connection – 'Tears on My Pillow', 'Sorry', 'Let's Dance', 'These Days'?

What comes next – 'Knock, Knock Who's There?', 'Beg Steal or Borrow', 'Let Me Be the One' …?

TOP 20

QUIZ 11 Answers

6 The titles have been No. 1 twice, but they are different songs (Johnny Nash/Kylie Minogue; Madonna/Justin Bieber; David Bowie/Five; Take That/Rudimental with Jess Glynne; Dan Caplen and Macklemore)

10 'Rock Bottom' (UK entries that finished second at the Eurovision Song Contest in the 1970s: 1970, 1972, 1975, 1977)

7 The Boomtown Rats (first four groups of musicians to play on the stage at Live Aid)

8 2002

9 All have had Top 40 hits with versions of the song 'Everlasting Love' (as have Love Affair, the cast of Casualty, Rex Smith & Rachel Sweet)

TOP **20**

All have had No. 1s that also feature Elton John ('Don't Go Breaking My Heart', 'Don't Let the Sun Go Down on Me', 'Sorry Seems to Be the Hardest Word', 'Ghetto Gospel')

1977

Diana Ross (female vocalists to register UK chart duets with Marvin Gaye beginning with the earliest)

(((**4**)))

34 (5+5+5+4+4+5+3+3)

(((**5**)))

Taylor (surnames of the classic line-up of Duran Duran)

QUIZ **12**

**What comes next – *Dangerously in Love, B'Day, I Am ...
Sasha Fierce* ...?**

**What's the connection – Edison Lighthouse, the Pretenders,
New Kids on the Block, Manic Street Preachers?**

**When was this – Chrissie Hynde married Jim Kerr; Wham's 'Choose
Life' T-shirts were a must have fashion item; Olly Murs was born?**

Who comes next – 'Marco', 'Merrick', 'Terry Lee' ...?

**Who's the connection – Ace, Roxy Music, Squeeze, Mike and
the Mechanics?**

What's the total – the number of singers to record as one of the Sugababes from their formation in 1998 to disbanding in 2011 ?

Who comes next – Janet, Randy, Michael ...?

When was this – the Blur v. Oasis chart battle makes the six o'clock news on the BBC; the duo Robson and Jerome had both the bestselling single and album of the year; 'Free as a Bird' became the first 'new' Beatles single since the beginning of the 1970s?

What's the specific connection – Wings, Lulu, Carly Simon, Shirley Bassey?

What comes next – 'Back Home', 'This Time (We'll Get It Right)', 'We've Got the Whole World at Our Feet' ...?

Six (Siobhan Donaghy, Keisha Buchanan, Mutya Buena, Heidi Range, Amelle Berrabah, Jade Ewen)

Marlon (the members of the Jackson family dynasty in ascending age from the youngest)

1995

Singers of the theme songs from the four James Bond films starring Roger Moore released in the 1970s (*Live and Let Die, The Man with the Golden Gun, The Spy Who Loved Me, Moonraker*)

'World in Motion' (official songs of England appearances at the FIFA World Cup since the first hit – 1970, 1982, 1986, 1990)

QUIZ 12 Answers

4 (the first four solo studio albums by Beyoncé)

The chart acts that recorded the first new No. 1s in the 1970s, 1980s, 1990s and 2000s ('Love Grows (Where My Rosemary Goes)', 'Brass in Pocket', 'Hangin' Tough', 'The Masses Against the Classes')

1984

Gary Tibbs (the order in which the members of Adam and the Ants are mentioned in the chorus of the group's Top 3 single 'Ant Rap')

Bands with whom Paul Carrack has recorded (Ace, 'How Long'; Roxy Music, *Manifesto*; Squeeze, *East Side Story* and 'Tempted'; several hits with Mike and the Mechanics)

QUIZ **13**

1

Who comes next – Queen, Bing Crosby, Pat Metheny Group …?

2

Who or what's the connection – 'Boys' by Britney Spears, 'One (Your Name)' by Swedish House Mafia, 'Feels' by Calvin Harris, 'Get Lucky' by Daft Punk?

3

What's the total – the titles of Adele's first three No. 1 albums?

4

What comes next – 'It's All Over Now', 'Little Red Rooster', 'The Last Time' …?

5

When was this – Bucks Fizz won the Eurovision Song Contest with 'Making Your Mind Up'; Phil Collins released *Face Value*, his first solo album; Ringo Starr married actress Barbara Bach?

6

What's the connection – *Peter Gabriel, Peter Gabriel, Peter Gabriel, Peter Gabriel*?

7

What comes next – 'Car', 'Scratch', 'Melt' …?

8

Who's missing – The Osmonds, Donny Osmond, Little Jimmy Osmond, ? , Donny and Marie Osmond?

9

What's the connection – 'Chicken', 'Deckchair', 'Jumbo Jet', 'Clothes'?

10

Who comes next – Shirley Jones, David Cassidy, Susan Dey ...?

TOP **20**

5

1981

6

The official titles of the first four solo albums by Peter Gabriel!

7

'Security' (the first four Peter Gabriel albums are all officially called *Peter Gabriel*, but in chronological order are also known by alternative names)

8

Marie Osmond (the chronological order in which members of the Osmond family first reached the Top 40)

9

The items that appear in the first four lines of the chorus of the Spitting Image's 1986 No. 1, 'The Chicken Song'

10

Danny Bonaduce (the actors who played the members of *The Partridge Family* beginning with the eldest)

QUIZ **13** Answers

TOP **20**

Mick Jagger (the order of David Bowie's charting collaborations in the 1980s: 'Under Pressure', 'Peace on Earth/Little Drummer Boy', 'This Is Not America', 'Dancing in the Street')

All four songs feature Pharrell Williams

65 (*19 + 21 + 25*)

'(I Can't Get No) Satisfaction' (the first four No. 1s by the Rolling Stones)

QUIZ **14**

1

Who comes next – Paul Young, Boy George, George Michael ...?

2

When was this – Little Mix win *The X Factor*; the Stone Roses announced they were to reform; *Sigh No More* by Mumford and Sons was named 'Best Album' at the BRIT Awards?

3

Who's the connection – Slik, Rich Kids, Visage, Ultravox?

4

What comes next – *Love Me Tender*, *Loving You*, *Jailhouse Rock* ...?

5

What's the total – the sum of No. 1 singles for individual members of the Spice Girls?

6

Who's missing – 'Jack', 'Stan', ?, 'Gus', 'Lee'?

7

What's the connection – 'A Lover's Concerto' by the Toys, 'Lady Lynda' by the Beach Boys, 'Plug in Baby' by Muse and 'Everything's Gonna Be Alright' by Sweetbox?

8

What comes next – 'Sudan', 'Japan', 'Milan' ...?

((9))

What's the total – of Barenaked Ladies' '... Week', DJ Shadow's '... Days', Gene Pitney's '... Hours from Tulsa', the Stranglers' '... Minutes' and So Solid Crew's '... Seconds'? (Careful with this one: the answer should similarly be in weeks, days, hours, etc.)

((10))

What's the connection – Joe Brown, Marty Wilde, Brian Poole, Brian Wilson?

5

Eight (Geri Halliwell 4, Melanie C 2, Emma Bunton 1, Melanie B 1, Victoria Beckham 0)

6

'Roy' (the names mentioned in order in the chorus of Paul Simon's '50 Ways to Leave Your Lover')

7

All four songs incorporate musical elements from Johann Sebastian Bach

8

'Yucután' (the four places named in the first verse of 'Hit Me with Your Rhythm Stick' by Ian Dury & the Blockheads

9

2 weeks, 5 minutes and 21 seconds ('One Week', 'Six Days', 'Twenty-four Hours from Tulsa', which is one day and when added to the 'Six Days' makes a week, '5 Minutes', '21 Seconds')

10

All have daughters who have also had hits (Sam Brown, Kim Wilde, Shelly and Karen Poole of Alisha's Attic, Carnie and Wendy Wilson of Wilson Phillips)

1 Simon Le Bon (the first four voices on Band Aid's 'Do They Know It's Christmas?')

2 2011

3 Midge Ure (sang with Slik, Rich Kids and Ultravox, co-wrote and co-produced the first five hits for Visage)

4 King Creole (Elvis Presley films in chronological order)

QUIZ **15**

www.whowhatwhen?

Who and what comes next – 'Aquarius'/'Ralph', 'Libra'/'Charles', 'Leo'/'Paul' ...?

What's the connection – Crystal Gayle, Gary Numan, Cliff Richard, songwriter Jimmy Webb?

When was this – Jimi Hendrix, Miles Davis and the Who were among the acts at the Isle of Wight Festival, David Bowie married Angela Barnett, the soundtrack to the summer was Mungo Jerry's No. 1 'In the Summertime'?

What comes next – *Purple Rain* (1984), *Parade* (1986), *Batman* (1989) ...?

What's the connection – McFly, Kenickie, T'Pau, Travis?

What's missing – 'The Girl Is Mine', 'Billie Jean', 'Beat It', ?, 'Thriller', 'P.Y.T. (Pretty Young Thing)'?

Who or what comes next – the Move, Electric Light Orchestra, Wizzard ...?

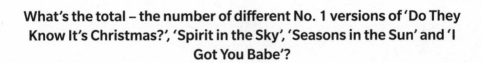

What's the total – the number of different No. 1 versions of 'Do They Know It's Christmas?', 'Spirit in the Sky', 'Seasons in the Sun' and 'I Got You Babe'?

When was this – Milli Vanilli returned their Grammy because they didn't sing on their records; Madonna's begins her 'Blond Ambition' tour with clothes designed by Jean-Paul Gaultier; Luciano Pavarotti was at No. 1 with *The Essential Pavarotti* and, along with José Carreras and Placido Domingo, *In Concert*?

What's the connection – Blancmange, Erasure, Sweet Dreams, A Teens?

Roy Wood as a solo artist (the order in which the singer/multi-instrumentalist/producer first charted in different guises ('Night of Fear', 1967; '10538 Overture', 1972; 'Ball Park Incident', 1972; 'Dear Elaine', 1973)

11 (Band Aid, Band Aid II, Band Aid 20, Band Aid 30; Norman Greenbaum, Doctor and the Medics, Gareth Gates featuring the Kumars; Terry Jacks, Westlife; Sonny & Cher, UB40 & Chrissie Hynde)

1990

Hit cover versions of Abba songs ('The Day Before You Came', Blancmange; 'Lay All Your Love on Me'/'SOS'/'Take a Chance on Me'/'Voulez-Vous', all on Erasure's 'Abba-esque EP'; 'Honey Honey', Sweet Dreams; 'Mamma Mia' and 'Super Trouper', A Teens)

QUIZ 15 Answers

'Cancer'/'Larry' (the members of the Floaters and their star signs in order according to the group's 1977 No. 1 'Float On')

Their birth surname is Webb – only Jimmy kept the surname (Brenda Gail Webb, Gary Anthony James Webb, Harry Rodger Webb, Jimmy Layne Webb)

1970

Graffiti Bridge (1990) (Prince/Prince & the Revolution albums that were also deemed soundtrack albums chronologically; *Parade* was the soundtrack for *Under the Cherry Moon*)

Took their names from fictitious TV or film characters (from *Back to the Future*; *Grease*; *Star Trek*; *Paris, Texas*)

'Wanna Be Startin' Something' (chronological UK hit singles from the album *Thriller*)

QUIZ **16**

1

What's the connection – Abba, ABC, Avicii featuring Aloe Blacc, Jonas Brothers?

2

When was this – Diana Ross missed a penalty at the opening ceremony of the World Cup in Chicago; Michael Jackson married Lisa Marie Presley; Wet Wet Wet spent 15 weeks at No. 1 with 'Love Is All Around'?

3

What comes next – 'a whisky drink', 'a vodka drink', 'a lager drink' …?

4

What's missing – *Screamadelica* by Primal Scream (1992), *Suede* by Suede (1993), ?, *Dummy* by Portishead (1995), *Different Class* by Pulp (1996)?

5

What's the connection – 'Bohemian Rhapsody' by Queen, 'Excerpt from a Teenage Opera' by Keith West, 'Song 2' by Blur, 'Annie's Song' by John Denver?

6

What's the total – the number of brothers in Sparks, members in the hit line-up of the Stylistics and members in the original hit line-up of Showaddywaddy, divided by the number of members in Steps? (Award yourself an extra point for naming which of these four acts had a hit song that contains the answer)

What comes next – 'Now That We've Found Love' by Heavy D & the Boyz, 'More Than Words' by Extreme, 'I'm Too Sexy' by Right Said Fred ...?

Who or what's the connection – 'She's a Windup' by Dr Feelgood, 'Watching the Detectives' by Elvis Costello, 'Stop Your Sobbing' by the Pretenders, 'Hey Lord Don't Ask Me Questions' by Graham Parker & the Rumour?

When was this – the 1962 American No. 1 'Monster Mash' by Bobby 'Boris' Pickett and the Crypt-Kickers finally made the UK charts; Peter Andre was born; the film *That'll Be the Day* starring David Essex and Ringo Starr was released?

![10]

What's the connection – 'Bat Out of Hell' by Meat Loaf, 'Red Rose Speedway' by Paul McCartney & Wings, 'Steve McQueen' by Prefab Sprout, 'Born This Way' by Lady Gaga?

TOP **20**

QUIZ 16 Answers

8

All four Top 40 hits were produced by Nick Lowe

7

'Let's Talk About Sex' by Salt-N-Pepa (the first four songs that only reached No. 2 thanks to Bryan Adams's ('(Everything I Do) I Do It for You') staying at No. 1 for 16 weeks

10

Album sleeves all feature motorbikes

9

1973

6

Three (2 + 5 + 8 ÷ 5 = 3); Showaddywaddy had a hit with 'Three Steps to Heaven')

TOP **20**

All have recorded different hit songs called 'SOS'

1994

'A cider drink' (the alcohol consumed in order in Chumbawamba's 'Tubthumping')

Elegant Slumming by M People (1994) (the first five winners of the Mercury Prize in order)

The titles of the songs do not feature in the lyrics

QUIZ **17**

www.whowhatwhen?

What's the connection – 911, Shed Seven, the Cure, Lisa Moorish (all in the 1990s)?

Who's missing – Hadley, Keeble, Kemp, Kemp ...?

When was this – Madonna made a guest appearance at the Eurovision Song Contest; Boyzone split for good; the original line-up of Sugababes reformed?

Who comes next – Lou Reed, Bono, Skye Edwards from Morcheeba ...?

What's the total – UK No. 1s by Abba, Brotherhood of Man and Bucks Fizz?

What's the connection – 'Psycho Killer' by Talking Heads, 'Hold on Tight' by ELO, 'Girls and Boys' by Prince, 'Denis' by Blondie?

What's the odd one out – 'Mouldy Old Dough', 'Trapped', 'Glad It's All Over', 'Space Oddity'?

What's the connection – 'Silver Star' by the Four Seasons, 'Don't Look Back in Anger' by Oasis, 'Does Your Mother Know' by Abba, 'Never Forget' by Take That?

When was this – the Smiths played their final gig; Lady Gaga was born; the Four Tops' Levi Stubbs provided the voice of Audrey II in *Little Shop of Horrors*?

Who comes next – Heather Small, Tom Jones, Heather Small …?

'Space Oddity' (the artists have military titles (Lieutenant Pigeon, Colonel Abrams, Captain Sensible) while David Bowie's hit has a military title in the lyrics (Major Tom)

Hit singles not sung by the usual lead singer(s) (Gerry Polci, Noel Gallagher, Björn Ulvaeus, Howard Donald)

1986

Lou Reed (the last four solo voices heard on the No. 1 version of Lou Reed's song 'Perfect Day' for BBC *Children in Need*)

QUIZ 17 Answers

Top 40 hits about Friday ('Party People ... Friday Night', 'She Left Me on Friday', 'Friday I'm in Love', 'Mr Friday Night')

Norman (the surnames of the 1980s line-up of Spandau Ballet)

2019

David Bowie (the first four solo voices heard on the No. 1 version of Lou Reed's song 'Perfect Day' for BBC *Children in Need*)

15 (Abba, nine; three each for the other two groups)

All four songs contain passages in the French language

QUIZ **18**

Who or what's the connection – 'Nothing Hurts Like Love' by Daniel Bedingfield, 'Numb' by Pet Shop Boys, 'Not a Dry Eye in the House' by Meat Loaf, 'If I Could Turn Back Time' by Cher?

Who comes next – Harman, Ward-Davies, Wilson, Dymond ...?

When was this – Kate Bush began her first tour called 'The Tour of Life'; the Sugarhill Gang's single 'Rapper's Delight' was considered the first 'rap' single to be a Top 40 hit; Gary Numan had No. 1 singles as both Tubeway Army and a solo artist?

Who or what is missing – John Lennon, ?, John Lennon, John Lennon?

What's the connection – Annie Lennox, Dido, Shane MacGowan, Alannah Myles?

When was this – the BBC launched Radio 1; the Monterey Pop Festival took place; Aretha Franklin recorded 'Respect'?

Who is missing – David Bowie, ?, Hunt Sales, Tony Sales?

What's the connection – 'The Bangin' Man' by Slade, 'Roadrunner' by Jonathan Richman, 'Raspberry Beret' by Prince, 'Give Peace a Chance' by the Plastic Ono Band

What comes next – 'Monday – late again', 'Tuesday – was so sad', 'Wednesday – met a girl' ...

What's the connection – the hit line-ups of Thompson Twins, the Walker Brothers, Three Dog Night and the Ritchie Family?

TOP **20**

6

1967

7

Reeves Gabrels (the four members of Tin Machine, which made two studio albums in 1989–91)

8

Songs all begin with count-ins

9

'Thursday – asks her for a date' (what happened to 'Horace' according to ELO's hit 'The Diary of Horace Wimp')

10

Their names contradict the composition of the act (three Thompson Twins; the Walker Brothers weren't brothers; seven members of Three Dog Night; the Ritchie Family weren't a family)

QUIZ **18** Answers

TOP 20

All written by Diane Warren

Amey (the surnames of the classic 1960s line-up of Dave Dee, Dozy, Beaky, Mick & Tich in order)

1979

St Winifred's School Choir (the UK No. 1 singles' artists immediately following the death of John Lennon: '(Just Like) Starting Over', 'There's No One Quite Like Grandma', 'Imagine', 'Woman')

All born on Christmas Day

QUIZ **19**

Who is missing – Michael Parkinson, Kenny Lynch, ? , Clement Freud, Christopher Lee, John Conteh?

What's the connection – the Spiders From Mars, Lemmy from Motörhead, Sandy Denny, Abba?

(((3)))

What's the total – of the numbers found in the titles of the 1978 album by Genesis that includes 'Follow You Follow Me'; the 1982 album by Mike Oldfield that includes 'Family Man' (as covered by Hall & Oates); the 1992 album by James that includes 'Born of Frustration' and 'Ring the Bells'; and the 2006 No. 1 compilation album by George Michael that includes 'Heal the Pain' recorded with Paul McCartney? (And for a bonus point, what is the title of the 2002 compilation by the Rolling Stones that includes the answer in its title?)

(((4)))

When was this – Jarvis Cocker was born; the Beatles played at the Cavern Club for the final time; the film *Summer Holiday* starring Cliff Richard opened in cinemas?

Who comes next – 'Monica (in my life)', 'Erica (by my side)', 'Rita (all I need)' ...?

What's the connection – the Beatles, Robbie Williams and Pet Shop Boys, Androids, Junior Vasquez?

(((7)))

Who's the connection – 'Jacky' by Marc Almond, 'Step into My Office, Baby' by Belle & Sebastian, 'On Silent Wings' by Tina Turner, 'Owner of a Lonely Heart' by Yes?

(((8)))

When was this – Jemini famously became the first UK act to score '*nul points*' at Eurovision; S Club (previously S Club 7) split up; Mick Jagger was knighted?

(((9)))

What's the total – of all the sisters in All Saints, the 1980s hit line-up of Five Star, the 'We Are Family' line-up of Sister Sledge and the 'I'm in the Mood for Dancing' line-up of the Nolans?

(((10)))

What's the connection – 'Love Action' by Human League, 'The Look of Love' by ABC, 'Hallelujah' by Happy Mondays, 'My Name Is Prince' by Prince?

6

All have had hit singles with 'Madonna' in the title ('Lady Madonna', 'She's Madonna', 'Do It with Madonna', 'If Madonna Calls')

7

All produced by Trevor Horn

8

2003

9

14 (Natalie and Nicole Appleton; Doris, Lorraine and Denise Pearson; Debbie, Kim, Kathy and Joni Sledge; Maureen, Anne, Bernie, Linda and Coleen Nolan)

10

Phil Oakey, Martin Fry, Shaun Ryder and Prince namecheck themselves in the songs

QUIZ 19 Answers

James Coburn (the famous faces, left to right, that appeared alongside Wings on the cover of *Band on the Run*)

All received blue plaques in 2017 (at Hull Paragon Station, Port Vale FC, Byfield Village Hall and Brighton Dome)

40 (*And Then There Were Three, Five Miles Out, Seven, Twenty Five*: 3 + 5 + 7 + 25 = 40); the Rolling Stones compilation is called *Forty Licks*

1963

'Tina (what I see)' (the first four names in the chorus of Lou Bega's 'Mambo No. 5')

QUIZ 20

www.whowhatwhen?

1

What's the connection –
'Curious', 'Radiance', 'Midnight
Fantasy', 'Believe'?

2

When was this – Jive Bunny
and the Mastermixers became
the third act in chart history
whose first three hits reached
No. 1; Band Aid II recorded a
new version of 'Do They Know
It's Christmas?'; compilation
albums were removed from the
mainstream albums chart?

3

Who is missing – Jimmy Young,
Liberace, ?, Les Baxter?

4

What's the connection – Tony
Iommi, Rowan Atkinson, Judie
Tzuke, Brian May in 1991?

5

What's the total – the Alarm's '...
Guns' divided by Jean Jacques
Smoothie's '... People' minus
the only hit for the Regents plus
Robert Miles's Top 3 follow-up to
'Children' featuring the vocals of
Maria Nayler? (The answer is the
title of a No. 1 from the 1980s –
award yourself an extra point if
you know who recorded it)

6

What comes next – 'Whole Lotta
Love', 'Yellow Pearl', 'The Wizard'
...?

7

When was this – Spice Girls launched Channel 5; Camila Cabello was born; Aqua's 'Barbie Girl' reportedly sold more than 8 million copies worldwide?

8

What's the connection – 'Bite Your Lip (Get Up and Dance)' by Elton John, 'Walking After You' by Foo Fighters, 'The Greatest Love of All' by George Benson, 'Hazy Shade of Winter' by the Bangles?

9

Who comes next – Jason Donovan, Keith Washington, Nick Cave …?

10

What's the connection – 'Against All Odds', 'That's My Goal', 'A Moment Like This', 'When You Believe'?

5

19 ('68 Guns' divided by '2 People' minus '7Teen' plus 'One & One' = 19; '19' was a hit for Paul Hardcastle)

6

'Now Get Out of That' (composed by Tony Gibber) (theme music for *Top of the Pops* in order, 1970–95)

7

1997

8

There was a different artist on the 'B' side of the original 7-inch single ('Chicago' by Kiki Dee, 'Beacon Light' by Ween, 'Ali's Theme' by Michael Masser, 'She's Lost You' by Joan Jett & the Blackhearts)

9

Robbie Williams (Top 40 duets by Kylie Minogue beginning with the earliest: 'Especially for You', 'If You Were with Me Now', 'Where the Wild Roses Grow', 'Kids')

10

The No. 1 songs of the first four UK *X Factor* winners (Steve Brookstein, Shayne Ward, Leona Lewis, Leon Jackson)

QUIZ **20** Answers

TOP **20**

They are the names of perfumes by Britney Spears

1989

Al Hibbler (four versions of 'Unchained Melody' were all in the Top 20 chart dated 17–23 June 1955)

They all featured on the No. 1 'The Stonk' by Hale & Pace and the Stonkers (along with Dave Gilmour, Cozy Powell, Roger Taylor and others – Rowan Atkinson played drums)

If you're a regular listener to 'PopMaster' on Ken Bruce's radio show, you'll know at the end of the year contestants who have scored maximum points are invited back to find the 'Champion of Champions'. Coming up are the type of questions these listeners might face. There are some extra points to be gained along the way. Proceed with extreme caution!

TOP

10

QUIZ 1

Under what pseudonym did Prince write the Bangles' hit 'Manic Monday'?

Two parts: Released at the very end of 2003, Robin Gibb provided guest vocals on 'My Lover's Prayer', one of two songs on a 2004 Top 5 double 'A' side by a singer-songwriter who appeared on the BBC's *Fame Academy* series – who is the singer-songwriter and what is the other song?

The American group Act One made its one and only Top 40 appearance in 1974 with which single?

What comes next – #2/2008 Sam Sparro; #2/1982 Stranglers; #2/1971 Rolling Stones; #2/1963 …?

The group Deee-Lite is best remembered for their 1990 Top 3 double 'A' side 'Groove Is in the Heart/What Is Love', but they did have one other Top 40 hit. Released the same year, it was also a double 'A' side – name both tracks on this other double 'A' side hit.

6

Name all three of the studio albums to date by the singer Halsey.

7

Following the early 1980s split of the Undertones, guitarist and songwriter John O'Neill formed a new group (which included brother and fellow Undertone Damian O'Neill). They had a Top 30 album in 1987 called *Babble*, from which the single 'Big Decision' just missed out on reaching the Top 40 (No. 43) – name the band.

8

Paul Gascoigne had a Top 3 hit in 1990 with 'Fog on the Tyne (Revisited)' billed as Gazza and Lindisfarne. But the footballer had one further Top 40 hit – what is its full title?

9

Which 1970s dance troupe was billed alongside Mike Batt on his 1975 Top 5 single 'Summertime City'?

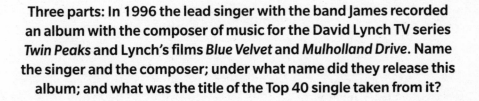

10

Three parts: In 1996 the lead singer with the band James recorded an album with the composer of music for the David Lynch TV series *Twin Peaks* and Lynch's films *Blue Velvet* and *Mulholland Drive*. Name the singer and the composer; under what name did they release this album; and what was the title of the Top 40 single taken from it?

That Petrol Emotion

'Geordie Boys (Gazza Rap)'

New Edition (the regular dance group on BBC One's *Seaside Special* for which 'Summertime City' was the theme song)

Tim Booth and Angelo Badalamenti; Booth and the Bad Angel (also the title of the album); 'I Believe'

QUIZ 1 Answers

Christopher (Christopher Tracy)

Alistair Griffin; 'Bring It On

'Tom the Peeper'

#2/63 Searchers (a sequence of No. 2 hits where the end of one title begins the next – 'Black and Gold', 'Golden Brown', 'Brown Sugar', 'Sugar and Spice')

'Power of Love', 'Deee-Lite Theme'

Badlands (2015), *Hopeless Fountain Kingdom* (2017), *Manic* (2020)

QUIZ **2**

1

Name the bass player with the La's who went on to form the band Cast?

2

In 1963, Gerry and the Pacemakers became the first chart act to have their first three hits all go to No. 1 in the same year. But what was the title of their fourth single, which stalled at No. 2 in 1964?

3

Echo and the Bunnymen first reached the Top 40 in 1981 with the song 'Crocodiles', but that wasn't the official title of the release. It was the lead song and airplay hit from a live four-track 12-inch EP – what was the title of this EP?

4

What was the name of the short-lived boyband in the first half of the 2000s, made up of singers who failed to be in the TV reality band One True Voice, but ended up having four hit singles (two more than One True Voice)?

5

Two parts: As they were coming towards the end of their chart run in the mid-1970s, Mud recruited a 'fifth' band member, Andy Ball, to play keyboards. He had previously been a member of a group that had its only Top 40 hit in 1974 – name that group and the title of the hit single.

6

Who or what is the connection – Kelly Rowland (2009); Sia (2011); Akon (2009); Sam Martin (2014)?

7

Two parts: Three 1980 singles by the Specials, 'Rat Race', 'Stereotype' and 'Do Nothing', were all officially listed with other songs as either double 'A' sides or the 'B' side. Name these three other songs; and what was the full official credit for 'Do Nothing'?

8

Name the singer who, in 1984, was in the charts at the same time as Lionel Richie with 'Stuck on You', but actually managed to chart higher than Richie's original version?

9

What's the connection – Status Quo in 1982; TLC in 1999; New Power Generation in 1995; Shalamar in 1982?

10

The country singer Billie Jo Spears had all three of her UK Top 40 hits in the mid-1970s – 'Blanket on the Ground' was the first, but can you name one of the other two?

TOP **10**

Have all been featured singers on No. 1 singles by David Guetta ('When Love Takes Over', 'Titanium', 'Sexy Chick', 'Lovers on the Sun')

'Rude Buoys Outa Jail' ('Rat Race'), 'International Jet Set' ('Stereotype'), 'Maggie's Farm' ('Do Nothing'); full credit for 'Do Nothing' is 'The Specials featuring Rico with the Ice Rink String Sounds'

Trevor Walters (Richie reached No. 12, Walters reached No. 9)

Singles that feature the names of TV comedies – 'Dear John', 'No Scrubs', 'The Good Life', 'Friends'

'What I've Got in Mind' (No. 4), 'Sing Me an Old Fashioned Song' (No. 34)

QUIZ 2 Answers

TOP 10

John Power

'I'm the One'

'Shine So Hard'

Phixx

Candlewick Green, 'Who Do You Think You Are?'

QUIZ **3**

Who provided guest vocals on the 2002 Top 20 single 'Scorpio Rising' by Death in Vegas?

The 1997 hit single 'Over and Over' by Puff Johnson featured on the soundtrack to which 1996 comedy film?

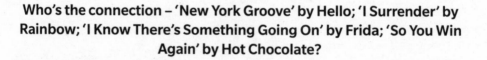

Who's the connection – 'New York Groove' by Hello; 'I Surrender' by Rainbow; 'I Know There's Something Going On' by Frida; 'So You Win Again' by Hot Chocolate?

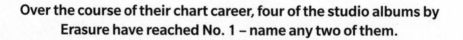

Over the course of their chart career, four of the studio albums by Erasure have reached No. 1 – name any two of them.

Which American heavy metal band had all five of its UK Top 40 songs in the first half of the 1990s – beginning with 'Silent Lucidity' in 1991 and ending with 'Bridge' in 1995?

6

The singer and model Nick Kamen is best remembered for his 1986 Top 5 single 'Each Time You Break My Heart' but reached the Top 40 on two other occasions in 1987–8 – name either of these other hits.

7

Alvin Stardust had four Top 40 hits in the early 1960s when he was known as Shane Fenton in Shane Fenton and the Fentones. 'I'm a Moody Guy' was the first – name one of the other three.

8

What was the stage name of Joseph Montanez, who had two Top 10 hits in the mid-1970s with 'Get Dancing' and 'I Wanna Dance Wit Choo (Doo Dat Dance)', recording as Disco Tex & the Sex-O-Lettes?

9

Three parts: What is the name of Alison Goldfrapp's partner in the duo Goldfrapp? What instrument did this partner play on the Tears for Fears album *Songs from the Big Chair*? And for which 2017 and 2020 nature documentary series did this partner compose the music?

10

Having left Ultravox in 1979, the singer John Foxx had four Top 40 solo singles – 'Underpass' in 1980 was the first, but can you name two of the other three?

'Walk Away', 'It's All Over Now', 'Cindy's Birthday'

Sir Monti Rock III

Will Gregory; Saxophone on 'I Believe' and 'The Working Hour'; *Spy In The Wild*

'No-One Driving', 'Burning Car' (both 1980), 'Europe (After the Rain)' (1981)

Liam Gallagher

The First Wives Club

All written by Russ Ballard (vocalist and guitarist with Argent)

The Innocents (1988), *Wild!* (1989), *Chorus* (1991), *I Say I Say I Say* (1994) (their compilation *Pop! The First 20 Hits* also reached No. 1)

Queensrÿche (five hit songs but six Top 40 appearances – 'Silent Lucidity' became a slightly bigger Top 40 hit on its 1992 reissue)

'Loving You Is Sweeter than Ever' (1987), 'Tell Me' (1988)

QUIZ 4

1

Which band had a Top 20 cover of Human League's 'Don't You Want Me' in 1992?

2

Two part: The singer Josiane Grizeau had a Top 10 single in 1971 with 'Un Banc, un Arbre, une Rue' – but under what name did she record this song and for which country did it win the Eurovision Song Contest in 1971?

3

What's the connection – 'Breathe' (2003), 'Baby Boy' (2003), 'What About Us' (2013), 'Dangerous Love' (2014)?

4

In 1986, which duo both wrote and released the original version of 'No More "I Love You"'s', the 1995 Top 3 hit for Annie Lennox?

5

One of the smaller Merseybeat groups of the early 1960s, the Big Three had both of their Top 40 hits in 1963 – name either of them.

6

What are the full names (first and surname) of the two male members in the pop vocal group Hear'Say, created from the reality TV show *Popstars* in 2001?

Which reggae singer took her version of the Police song 'The Bed's Too Big Without You' into the Top 40 in 1981?

The short-lived female vocal group Vanilla had both of their Top 40 hits in the late 1990s – name either of them.

Jim Capaldi had his biggest solo hit in 1975 with a Top 5 cover of the song 'Love Hurts', but he'd had one other Top 40 hit the year before – what is the title of this debut solo hit?

What's the connection – Freddie Mercury (1987 and 1992), Jennifer Rush (1989), Sarah Brightman (1992), Elton John (1996), and what are the songs? (Beware – the year is especially important in one case!)

TOP 10

QUIZ 4 Answers

6 'It's All Up to You,'

8 'No Way No Way' (1997), 'True to Us' (1998)

7 Sheila Hylton

9 Danny Foster, Noel Sullivan

10 Top 40 duets with opera singers (Montserrat Caballé, 'Barcelona'; Placido Domingo, 'Til I Loved You'; José Carreras, 'Amigos Para Siempre (Friends for Life)'; Luciano Pavarotti, 'Live Like Horses'; If you answered Andrea Bocelli and 'Time to Say Goodbye (Con te Partirò)' for Sarah Brightman you're wrong – that was 1997!)

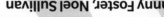

TOP 10

The Farm

Séverine, Monaco

All Top 3 hits featuring guest appearances from Sean Paul (Blu Cantrell, Beyoncé, Saturdays, Fuse ODG)

The Lover Speaks

'Some Other Guy', 'By the Way'

QUIZ **5**

Under what name did the singer born David Emmanuel record his mid-1980s Top 20 hit 'Police Officer'?

What shared song title has provided different hits for Shakespear's Sister in 1992, Ricky Martin in 2005 and Cheryl in 2014?

A 1997 hit single by Babybird has the same title as the name of a chart act that reached No. 1 in 1998 – what is that shared title/ name?

What's the connection – Blur, the Clash, the Verve, Fela Kuti?

Name both the main act and the featured guest group that recorded the 2003 hit single 'The Golden Path'.

Allowing for the fact that 'Philadelphia Freedom' is officially credited as the Elton John Band, Elton John's first official Top 40 collaboration came in 1976 with Kiki Dee on 'Don't Go Breaking My Heart' – but what was his second Top 40 credited collaboration, which reached the charts in 1981? (Award a couple of bonus points for the connection to the 'Philadelphia Freedom' single.)

Three parts: Name the singer who was lead vocalist with the Buzzcocks before their chart success; the band he formed on leaving the Buzzcocks; and the 1978 single that missed out on being this band's only Top 40 hit when it stalled at No. 41.

In 1992, Mike Oldfield had his fourth and final Top 10 single with which track?

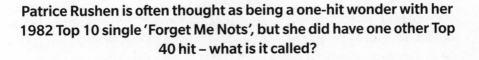

Patrice Rushen is often thought as being a one-hit wonder with her 1982 Top 10 single 'Forget Me Nots', but she did have one other Top 40 hit – what is it called?

Which American group had a hit in 2003 with their version of the Billy Idol song 'White Wedding'?

'I Saw Her Standing There', Elton John Band featuring John Lennon and the Muscle Shoals Horns (Top 40 in 1981, it was a live recording from 1974 that had previously featured as the 'B' side of 'Philadelphia Freedom')

Howard Devoto; Magazine; 'Shot by Both Sides'

'Sentinel' (full title: 'Sentinel (Single Restructure)' as it was a restructured shorter version of the opening track from his album *Tubular Bells II*)

'I Was Tired of Being Alone'

The Murderdolls (side project of Slipknot drummer Joey Jordison)

QUIZ 5 Answers

Smiley Culture

'I Don't Care'

Cornershop (Babybird's single 'Cornershop' was a Top 40 hit in May 1997; Cornershop reached No. 1 with 'Brimful of Asha' in February 1998)

Members of each of these bands/Fela Kuti's band came together to form 'supergroup' the Good, the Bad & the Queen (Damon Albarn/ Blur; Paul Simonon/Clash; Simon Tong/Verve; Tony Allen/Fela Kuti)

The Chemical Brothers featuring the Flaming Lips

QUIZ **6**

1

What are the names of the two founding members of Kraftwerk?

2

Two parts: Who sang vocals alongside Boy George on Culture Club's single 'Church of the Poison Mind' and what was the title of her own 1984 Top 40 solo hit?

3

Three parts: Name the song that marked Nicole Kidman's debut on the Top 40; name her singing partner on that song; and give the full artist credit and song title of that singing partner's Top 10 debut four years before Nicole.

4

Which band released one single a month for every month in 1992 (each single spent just one week in the Top 40)?

5

The singer Susan Fassbender had her only hit single in 1981 with which song?

6

Separated by 30 years and 20 years, name all three chart acts/ artists from 1961, 1991 and 2011 to have Top 40 hit singles with different songs called 'Jealousy'?

7

What is the name of the record label founded by George Harrison that had its first hit in 1974 with the single 'Costafine Town' by Splinter?

8

Name both the song and the Irish group billed on the 1992 Top 10 double 'A' side single along with Manic Street Preachers version of 'Theme from M.A.S.H. (Suicide Is Painless)'.

9

'The Lion Sleeps Tonight' was No. 1 in 1982 for Tight Fight, but the song had already been a Top 40 hit in both the 1960s and 1970s for two other chart acts – name both of these acts.

10

The singer and jazz musician Curtis Stigers is best known for his two Top 10 hits 'I Wonder Why' and 'You're All that Matters to Me', but he did have two further Top 40 hits in the 1990s – name both of these.

TOP **10**

5

'Twilight Café'

6

Billy Fury (1961), Pet Shop Boys (1991), Will Young (2011)

7

Dark Horse

8

'(Everything I Do) I Do It for You' by Fatima Mansions

9

The Tokens (1961–2), Dave Newman (1972)

10

'Never Saw a Miracle', 'This Time'

QUIZ **6** Answers

TOP **10**

Ralf Hütter, Florian Schneider

Helen Terry; 'Love Lies Lost'

'Come What May'; Ewan McGregor;
'Choose Life' by PF Project featuring
Ewan McGregor ('Come What May'
was in the charts two months before
Nicole's No. 1 duet with Robbie
Williams)

The Wedding Present (the January,
March and May singles both
managed a second week within the
Top 75)

QUIZ 7

1

Who famously turned up on *Top of the Pops* playing keyboards on a performance of 'Get It On' by T.Rex?

2

Two parts: A well-known TV presenter made an appearance early in their career as a dancer in a 1991 video to a Kylie Minogue single – who is the presenter and what was the single?

3

What's the connection – Midnight Oil, Sonny & Cher, Blur, Big Country/Runrig?

4

As of the end of 2019, what is the title of the only No. 1 by Jay-Z where the rapper is the lead artist rather than a featured artist?

5

Terry Jacks had solo hits in 1974 with 'Seasons in the Sun' and 'If You Go Away', but he had previously been part of a Canadian group that had a Top 10 hit in 1970 called 'Which Way You Goin' Billy?' – name the group.

6

Having had hits in the mid-1980s, the group Propaganda (with a new lead singer, Betsi Miller) had one further Top 40 single in 1990 – what was it called?

7

In the week the Hollies reached No. 1 in 1988 with a re-release of 'He Ain't Heavy He's My Brother', the song was also in the lower reaches of the Top 40 for another chart artist – who?

8

Three parts: Who was the first chart act/artist to hold all three Top 3 spots on the UK singles chart; what was the year; what were the songs?

9

Often considered the first all-female rock band to sign to a major label, what is the name of the American group who had a UK hit in 1965 called 'Can't You Hear My Heart Beat?'?

10

The Irish singer Brian Kennedy had a Top 40 hit in 1997 with his version of which World Party song?

5

The Poppy Family

6

'Heaven Give Me Words'

7

Bill Medley (his version entered the Top 40 the same week as the Hollies re-release, peaked at No. 25, and was at No. 38 in the week the Hollies reached No. 1)

8

Justin Bieber; 2016; 'What Do You Mean' (No. 3) 'Sorry' (No. 2) 'Love Yourself' (No. 1)

9

Goldie and the Gingerbreads

10

'Put the Message in the Box'

1

Elton John

2

Davina McCall; 'Word Is Out'

3

Each chart act has had a member that has held political office (Peter Garrett, including Minister for the Environment; Sonny Bono, including Mayor of Palm Springs; Dave Rowntree, Norfolk County Councillor; Pete Wishart, SNP Shadow Leader of the House of Commons)

4

'Run This Town' (2009) (billed as Jay-Z featuring Rihanna and Kanye West; other No. 1s 'Déjà Vu' by Beyoncé featuring Jay-Z (2006), 'Umbrella' by Rihanna featuring Jay-Z (2007))

QUIZ **8**

By what name is the singer born Melissa Viviane Jefferson best known?

Joy Division are often considered one-hit wonders for 'Love Will Tear Us Apart', but one other song by the group reached the Top 40 – name that song.

'Let Me Try Again' was the title of a Top 5 single and Top 40 album in 1975 for which Welsh singer?

The puppet duo Zig and Zag had a Top 10 hit in 1994 with 'Them Girls Them Girls' but made one other Top 40 appearance in the summer of 1995 with which single?

Three parts: Name the lead singer with late 1980s band Then Jericho; the 2003 reality TV show he briefly appeared in; the singer who ended up winning that TV show.

The American group Dynasty made its only UK Top 40 appearance in 1979 with a Top 20 single that had the subtitle '(But I Can't Help Myself)' – what is its full title?

What is the name of the female duo that had both their Top 40 hits in 1995 with the songs 'Independent Love Song' and 'I Wanna Be Free (to Be with Him)'?

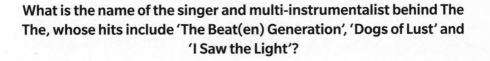

As the leader of Boogie Box High, George Michael's cousin had a Top 10 version of the Bee Gees' 'Jive Talkin'' in 1987 – who is he? (And just for fun, what other hit 1980s musicians are said to have contributed to the single?)

What's the connection – Bronski Beat, Carly Simon, Annie Lennox, Mis-Teeq?

What is the name of the singer and multi-instrumentalist behind The The, whose hits include 'The Beat(en) Generation', 'Dogs of Lust' and 'I Saw the Light'?

QUIZ **8** Answers

Matt Johnson

All have had hit singles called 'Why?'/'Why?'

Andros Georgiou (and reportedly uncredited George Michael, Nick Heyward of Haircut 100 and Mick Talbot of the Style Council)

Scarlet

Lizzo

'Atmosphere'

Tammy Jones

'Hands Up! Hands Up!'

Mark Shaw; *Reborn in the USA*; Tony Hadley

'I Don't Want to Be a Freak (But I Can't Help Myself)'

QUIZ **9**

1

Under what name did the R&B singer born Elgin Lumpkin record his 1997 Top 10 version of Prince's 'When Doves Cry'?

2

Which of the hit singles by Five Star makes a passing reference to David Bowie in its lyric?

3

Three parts: Name the artist who made his UK chart debut as a guest on Drake's 2012 Top 40 hit 'Crew Love'; either of his own 2016 Top 10 singles that featured Daft Punk; Daft Punk's own chart debut from 1997.

4

From 1962 to 2019, just two months of the year have failed to appear in the title of any Top 40 hit single – name both of these months. (Names of months that appear in titles with a different meaning. e.g. as a verb, proper noun, etc., don't count.)

5

Name both the British actor and the American vocal group backing him who had a Top 40 hit in 1998 with a cover of the Hall & Oates song 'She's Gone'.

6

Three parts: Name the female vocal group that sang backing vocals on Lou Reed's 'Walk on the Wild Side' and Mott the Hoople's 'Roll Away the Stone';

the title of their one and only Top 40 single; the 1970s chart star who co-wrote that hit?

Name both the 1980 hit duet billed as Olivia Newton-John and Cliff Richard and the 1995 hit duet billed as Cliff Richard and Olivia Newton-John.

As of the end of 2019, Matt Goss of Bros has had four Top 40 solo hits – name any two of these four.

What's the connection – 'Tempertemper'/'Making Up Again'; 'Heart of Stone'/Baby I Love You OK!'; 'Pillow Talk'/'Y Viva España'; 'Romeo'/'To Be with You'? (Bonus points for the names in the answer)

Brian Setzer, formerly of the Stray Cats, made his only Top 40 appearance as Brian Setzer Orchestra in 1999 with which single?

Matthew Marsden and Destiny's Child

Thunderthighs; 'Central Park Arrest'; Lynsey de Paul (co-written with John Cameron)

'Suddenly' (1980) (original sleeve and official charts credit 'Olivia Newton-John and Cliff Richard', the single's label credits 'Olivia Newton-John with Cliff Richard'); 'Had to Be' (1995)

'The Key' (1995), 'If You Were Here Tonight' (1996), 'I'm Coming with Ya' (2003), 'Fly' (2004)

(((**9**)))

Top 40 songs by pairs of chart acts that share the same name (Goldie, Kenny, Sylvia, Mr Big)

(((**10**)))

'Jump Jive an' Wail'

QUIZ **9** Answers

TOP **10**

Ginuwine

'Rain or Shine' (the song mentions Major Tom as a superhero)

The Weeknd, 'Starboy' (No. 2), 'I Feel It Coming' (No. 9), 'Da Funk/ Musique'

March, August (August was in the title of a single by Robin Gibb – 'August October' – but it only reached No. 45)

QUIZ **10**

1

Which Australian singer-songwriter was the co-founder, lead vocalist and main songwriter of the group Icehouse?

2

Two parts: The 1980 Top 40 single 'You Gotta Be a Hustler If You Wanna Get On' by Sue Wilkinson was released on Cheapskate Records, established by a songwriter and bass player in one of the most successful bands of the 1970s – who is he and in which band did he have hits?

3

What is the full title of the 1998 Top 40 Christmas single by Fat Les?

4

Christina Aguilera provided guest vocals on 'Say Something', a 2014 hit for which American duo?

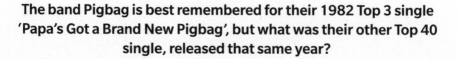

5

The band Pigbag is best remembered for their 1982 Top 3 single 'Papa's Got a Brand New Pigbag', but what was their other Top 40 single, released that same year?

The 1969 single 'No Mule's Fool' was the first of four hit singles for which group?

The American boyband trio EYC had its most successful year in the UK charts in 1994 with four Top 40 entries – name one of them.

What's the connection – Europe's singer, Showaddywaddy's drummer, the talking bit in 'Whispering Grass', Top 3 hit for Supergrass?

In 2009, the classical cross-over singer Katherine Jenkins just scraped into the Top 75 with her version of a 2003 No. 1 by an American rock band – name both the song and the band.

The singles 'Undone – The Sweater Song' in 1995 and 'Pork and Beans' in 2008 are the first and last of eight UK Top 40 hits for which American band?

'The Way You Work It', 'Number One', 'Black Book', 'One More Chance' (their 1993 debut 'Feelin' Alright' reached its chart peak of No. 16 in January 1994, but had been a Top 40 entry at the end of 1993)

Shakespeare (Joey TEMPEST, ROMEO (& Juliet) Challenger, (The Merry Wives of) WINDSOR Davies, RICHARD III)

'Bring Me to Life' by Evanescence

Weezer

QUIZ 10 Answers

Iva Davies

Jim Lea; Slade

'Naughty Christmas (Goblin in the Office)'

A Great Big World

'The Big Bean'

Family

*S*urprise! You thought it was all over – but no! As fans of *'Popmaster' on BBC Radio 2 are aware, a certain type of question has given birth to a prized T-shirt. Can you guess the years in question for the following months. Will you get in spot on? Or will you be 'One Year Out'?*

THE
FINALE

THE **FINALE** One Year Out

JANUARY: In which year did these three songs all enter the Top 40 in this month – 'Heart of Glass' by Blondie, 'King Rocker' by Generation X, 'Every Night' by Phoebe Snow?

(((4)))

FEBRUARY: In which year were these three singles Top 3 hits this month – the double 'A' side 'Ebony Eyes'/'Walk Right Back' by the Everly Brothers, 'Are You Lonesome Tonight?' by Elvis Presley, 'You're Sixteen' by Johnny Burnette?

(((3)))

MARCH: In which year did these three singles all enter the Top 40 in this month – 'When I Kiss You (I Hear Charlie Parker Playing)' by Sparks, 'Wake Up Boo!' by the Boo Radleys, the double 'A' side 'High and Dry/Planet Telex' by Radiohead?

APRIL: In which year did these three songs all enter the Top 40 in this month – 'I Need a Man' by Eurythmics, 'When Will You (Make My Telephone Ring)' by Deacon Blue, 'I Want You Back' by Bananarama?

MAY: In which year were these three songs Top 3 hits this month – 'I Won't Let You Down' by PhD, 'Only You' by Yazoo, 'A Little Peace' by Nicole?

JUNE: In which year did these three songs all enter the Top 40 in this month – 'Skweeze Me, Pleeze Me' by Slade, 'Goodbye Is Just Another Word' by the New Seekers, 'Life on Mars' by David Bowie?

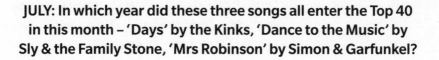

JULY: In which year did these three songs all enter the Top 40 in this month – 'Days' by the Kinks, 'Dance to the Music' by Sly & the Family Stone, 'Mrs Robinson' by Simon & Garfunkel?

AUGUST: In which year were these three songs Top 3 hits this month – 'I Don't Care' by Ed Sheeran and Justin Bieber, 'Beautiful People' by Ed Sheeran featuring Khalid, 'Senorita' by Shawn Mendes and Camila Cabello?

THE **FINALE** One Year Out

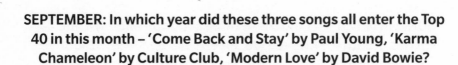

SEPTEMBER: In which year did these three songs all enter the Top 40 in this month – 'Come Back and Stay' by Paul Young, 'Karma Chameleon' by Culture Club, 'Modern Love' by David Bowie?

OCTOBER: In which year were these three albums Top 3 hits this month – *Life for Rent* by Dido, *Permission to Land*' by the Darkness, *Absolution* by Muse?

NOVEMBER: In which year were these three singles Top 3 hits this month – 'Missing' by Everything but the Girl, 'Gangsta's Paradise' by Coolio featuring L.V., the double 'A' side 'I Believe'/'Up on the Roof' by Robson and Jerome?

DECEMBER: In which year did these three songs all enter the Top 40 in this month – 'September' by Earth, Wind & Fire, 'I'll Put You Together Again' by Hot Chocolate, 'Song for Guy' by Elton John?

ANSWERS THE **FINALE**

January: 1979 February: 1961 March: 1995 April:1988 May: 1982 June: 1973 July: 1968 August: 2019 September: 1983 October: 2003 November: 1995 (Again! Sneaky! Did we catch you out?) December: 1978